WHEN
YOUR
CHILD...

WHEN
YOUR
CHILD...

**John M. Drescher
and Others**

Adapted from
Christian Living magazine
by its editor, David E. Hostetler

HERALD PRESS
Scottdale, Pennsylvania
Kitchener, Ontario
1986

Library of Congress Cataloging-in-Publication Data
When your child—

Bibliography: p.
1. Child rearing   2. Parent and child.
3. Children—Conduct of life.   4. Youth—Conduct of
life.   I. Drescher, John M.   II. Hostetler, David E.
HQ769.W495   1986   649'.1   86-12077
ISBN 0-8361-3416-8

Contents

WHEN YOUR CHILD . . .

WHEN YOUR CHILD ...

WHEN YOUR CHILD ...

Editor's Preface

Parenting, like weather forecasting, is not an exact science. Neither can be totally predictable in its outcomes. Yet the need for fairly reliable weather previews and good family management continues.

This book, though not disdaining the assistance of the human sciences, takes a commonse approach to raising children. In it, parents tell parents how they coped with specific problems that arose in their own families.

Beginning with the time a child comes into a family and running through childhood discontent, fear of being abandoned, misbehavior in church, and teenage pregnancy, to a rejection of parental values, the chapters in *When Your Child . . .* appear roughly in chronological order.

Each account deals with a specific problem: losing a pet, going to the hospital, stealing, playing with guns, and many more. Though problem-centered, the book is not pessimistic. It shows how parents accepted responsibility for problems and worked their way through them, aided by faith and Christian community.

Except for chapter 1, the essays in this book first appeared as articles in *Christian Living* magazine, issued monthly by

Mennonite Publishing House, Scottdale, Pennsylvania.

To then editor, J. Lorne Peachey, and associate editor, Helen Alderfer, goes credit for the hard work of conceptualizing, soliciting, and processing the series. It was their vision that allowed this down-to-earth compilation to come into being.

—David E. Hostetler, Editor
Christian Living Magazine

WHEN
YOUR
CHILD...

1

John M. Drescher # When Your Child First Joins the Family

Our daughter Rose and her husband, Rich, were just given a beautiful gift from God in the person of a baby daughter, Ginger. And I ask myself, what is it that I would like to say to Rose and Rich as they begin their family? What surfaces as uppermost to me now, as a father and grandfather?

I know how swiftly the growing years will pass. The diaper days, the muddy shoes, the messy rooms, and the encroachments on time will soon be gone. One stage of childhood quickly moves into another, often before parents are prepared. Sometimes I want to shout to parents, "Please take time now to relax, have fun, and enjoy your child." The most common statement heard at family retreats is, "If I had it to do over, I would take more time with my child." Love is really spelled T-I-M-E.

Beyond the sudden shift of schedules, the nights awake, the fixing of formula, and the abundant adjustments a baby brings to a home, there is the constant challenge to choose and cling to proper priorities. Today, several such priorities push themselves into my mind as the most pressing ones.

John M. Drescher, Harrisonburg, Virginia, and his wife Betty (Keener) are the parents of five grown children. His books include *Meditations for the Newly Married* (Herald Press), *If I Were Starting My Family Again* (Abingdon Press), and *Seven Things Children Need* (Herald Press).

Priority 1. Put God in his proper place. The privilege of parent-hood is God-given. According to the psalmist, children are a heritage from the Lord. He observes further that unless the Lord builds a home, the effort is in vain. (See Psalm 127.) Parents need the foundation of faith in God which will give support through all of life—childhood, adolescence, young adult, middle age, old age—and all the crises which come in every family.

A young man serving in one of the world's trouble spots was asked by a friend, "How is it possible for you to serve here? Aren't the temptations terrific?"

"Yes," he replied, "the temptations are tremendous. But my parents taught me to trust in God. I can still hear my father and mother's prayers when I left home. They prayed for God's presence to go with me and for God to help me remain faithful to the teachings they sought to give me. I know my family is praying fervently for me every day."

In one of the earliest statements of child guidance, the Scriptures tell us that the task and privilege of teaching the child is not a hit-and-miss method. "These commandments that I give you today are to be upon your hearts. Impress them or your children. Talk about them when you sit at home and when you walk along the road, when you lie down and when you get up" (Deuteronomy 6:6-7).

Three important principles are pointed to in this passage:

First, parents are to be right with God themselves. Parents must not only *know* the way and *show* the way. They must first *go* the way.

Second, the primary responsibility for training children is not on the school or society, or even the church, but on parents. Canon Lumb wrote: "Religious words have value to the child only as experience in the home gives them meaning."

Third, instruction is to be constant. To talk about God and his will when we arise, retire, sit down, or walk in the way does not mean incessant chatter about religion. It means only that the parents' own faith is so vital that it is natural, in all circumstances and relationships of life, to speak of God and relate to him.

If, as Henry Drummond wrote, "The family circle is the supreme conductor of Christianity," then we must hallow the daily duties and delights of family life with the touch of the divine. The family is to be the demonstration of godly living.

Priority 2. Keep the husband-wife love strong. When the first child arrives the marriage enters a crisis. Will the husband and wife keep their own love relationship primary or will one or both give primary attention to the child? A husband said it this way: "I had a wonderful wife until our first child was born. Then Jean became more of a mother than a mate."

If husband and wife keep their own love relationship strong and vital and continue to pay primary attention to each other, the child will reap all the blessings and benefits of their love. But if their own love relationship takes second place, not only will the marriage suffer but also the child.

Therefore, as parents, we should remember that the marriage partnership is permanent while parenthood is passing. Keep the partnership in good repair and the parenting will tend to take care of itself. If, however, the partnership weakens, the very structure which supports the child erodes. There is no satisfactory substitute for this primary support and strength.

Dr. David Goodman says it well in his excellent book, *A Parent's Guide to the Emotional Needs of Children.* "Your baby will smile at you and later at the world, if you two will never cease smiling to each other. No fact of child training is truer or more important than this."

This means that parents must replenish each other's affections and fulfill each other's need for love, so that this mutual overflow of love will envelop the child and enlarge the child's own love, security, and significance. The increased domestic demands on the wife calls for additional help from the husband in household and child-rearing tasks—a partnership in parenting.

When love between mother and father is not known and felt, the child has lost the most essential ingredient for the understanding of love and how to love. When love is seen and sensed between parents, the child has a good basis for beginning to understand the sanctity of sex, the meaning of marriage, and the reality of God's love. When love is present between mother and father, the child has a kind of inherent understanding of what is needed and proper in the forming of friendships, in dating and courtship, and later in the establishing of one's own home and family.

Only when a husband and wife meet each other's needs in satisfying ways do they free themselves to give wholesome love for the child.

Priority 3. Remember the power of example. It is true one example is worth more than many words. Hohman writes in *As the Twig Is Bent,* "The most potent influence in child culture is imitation." From the earliest moments the child is a copycat. This is a primary way of learning. Copying covers every area of life. Play is patterned after parent's practice. As surely as parents provide for the child's clothes and food, they form the child's habits and behavior by their own example.

Years ago John Webb wrote: "Whether it be for good or evil, the education of the child is principally derived from its own observation of the actions, words, voice, and looks of those with whom it lives."

Parents must be what they want their child to become. Moral values are imparted as the child sees them. The attitudes of the child are usually the reflection of the parents' own behavior—their attitude toward persons and material things, and their response to all kinds of happenings and situations.

Since values and beliefs are more caught than taught, the attitudes of parents and the atmosphere of the home are of tremendous importance. The atmosphere of the home cannot be seen or touched. But it is felt. It is a thing of the spirit. And no photographer's film is as sensitive as the spirit of the child. The images which lodge there determine the direction and destiny of the child. If the atmosphere is one of love, the child absorbs that love. If it is an atmosphere of trust, acceptance, and security the child moves forward in confidence and with a sense of worth.

Therefore, from the first day parents ought to pay particular attention to the atmosphere and attitudes of the home.

Years ago a wise mother wrote: "Do you ask what will educate your child? Your example will educate your child, your conversation with your friends, the business your child sees you transact, the likes and dislikes your child hears you express—these will educate your child. Your attitude and life, your house, your table will educate your child. Education goes on every instant of time. You neither stop it nor turn its course. What these have a tendency to make your child, that your child will be all of life." (Adapted)

Priority 4. Unfold rather than mold. From the day the child is born, parents begin to prepare the child and themselves for letting go. Just as growing up is the goal of childhood, a child's independence is the goal of good parenting. The primary part of parenthood does not consist of bringing a child to birth but in providing the relationships and opportunities for the child to become the contributing person God intends.

The parent's task is not so much to mold the child as to provide the conditions in which the child can unfold. The baby enters the world as a bundle of possibilities. In the early months and years the child develops more rapidly than ever again. Not only is physical growth dramatic but in every way the child's development is dynamic. For example, according to some studies, by the end of a child's first four years as much as half of the child's lifetime intelligence is already achieved. Another 30 percent is reached by the age of eight.

Intelligence means the ability to handle mentally the information received. Knowledge will, of course, continue to increase as long as the child keeps learning, but the capacity to handle information is fully half established before starting school. Therefore what happens very early determines to a large extent how the child will develop later.

From the start parents should realize that each stage of development is preparation for the following stage. This is difficult to remember because the years move so swiftly. Opportunities soon pass. The early years of closeness, correction, and loving relationships prepare the child for the middle childhood years. At that stage the child is guided more by the great drive to become like those the child admires. Middle childhood, between ages 6 and 12, is the time to prepare the child for adolescence. The child who knows what to expect on entering adolescence is the child who is sure and confident. Guidance for dating, courtship, and marriage needs to be given long before the child enters these experiences.

Priority 5. Let there be joy. One final word must be said. A child thrives and grows when parents are happy and when parents enter into the thrill of the child's enjoyments and excitements. A child can get along on limited creature comforts if the home is a happy, fun-filled family. A child doesn't need toys, clothes, and rich food half as much as the companionship of happy, loving, light-spirited parents.

I shall never forget the young married man at a retreat who spoke glowingly of his father. "When we worked with Dad as boys," he said, "he expected us to work hard. But when we played he played with as much enthusiasm as any of us. We had the feeling our dad really enjoyed us."

There is nothing as sad as a dispirited child who has lost the spark of joy. And there is nothing more delightful than to see a child's eyes filled with happiness.

2

Sara Wengerd When Your Child
Is No Longer
the Baby

Heidi stood before the hospital nursery window, feet planted firmly, glaring at her new sister behind the glass. Later, our 2½-year-old announced she did not want Mother to bring "that baby" home. That was our first indication that we had a lot to do in the slow, painful process of turning sibling rivalry into sisterly love.

Surely, fear of losing parental love was an issue for Heidi as it must be for any child learning to share affection. Born to us after six years of marriage, the loss of a premature baby, and following a complicated pregnancy, Heidi seemed to be a special gift. We became doting parents, devoting much of our time to playing with and enjoying her. She grew accustomed to receiving much attention and developed few skills in playing alone.

Before she was two, John and I decided to have a second baby to provide Heidi some of the fun and companionship we had enjoyed growing up with brothers and sisters. This second pregnancy was complicated as well, so the doctor recommended activity limitations and some bedrest. Heidi could not

Sara Wengerd, Salisbury, Pennsylvania, mother of two, is a volunteer, giving home-care to the elderly in her community. Her hobbies include gardening, travel, reading, and free-lance writing.

understand my immobility and must have felt uneasy when I
was irritable and apprehensive. I could not lift her and so I encouraged her to sit beside me for reading and games. She became accustomed to my undivided attention for long periods
of time.

Kristin was born two days after Christmas by cesarean sec-
tion. My mother came to spend the week with Heidi and
found her to be agitated and uncooperative. She refused to
allow Grandma to put her to bed, insisting that this was
Daddy's task. She seemed to be saying, "Mommy, you've left
me, and I'm not going to accept grandma as a substitute."

We tried to think of ways to communicate to Heidi that
there was still a bond between us, even though I was absent. I
made a tape of her favorite songs and stories, which proved to
be a great comfort to her. Small gifts were hidden around the
house, and I phoned her each day to reveal a new hiding place.
John brought her to the hospital for a visit, but she was cool
and distant, shrugging off my embrace as if I was a stranger.
Although I had read that this was the kind of reaction to expect, when it actually occurred I felt hurt and guilty for the rift
in our normally close relationship.

The first six weeks of our new life together as a family of
four are but a blur of diaper changes, colic, temper tantrums,
and utter exhaustion. Baby Kristin slept peacefully during the
day but developed discomfort in the evenings and often cried
until 2:00 a.m. Although John and I shared night duty, we
were both tired when morning came.

We expected Heidi to be jealous of Kristin, and we were
eager to protect her from being upstaged by the baby. But we
were not prepared for the strength and duration of her reaction or for our own feelings of anger toward her.

At first Heidi's negative feelings were expressed in indirect
ways: temper tantrums, unreasonable demands, regressive be-

havior. She seemed particularly threatened when I nursed Kristin, so I read to her at feeding time.

Later, she vented her hostility directly by biting the baby's fingers or by hitting her. When she hugged Kristin, she gritted her teeth, and she handled the baby roughly when we bathed her together. I found myself spanking her frequently or lashing out at her verbally. She turned to her father for comfort and showed a definite preference for his company.

In his book *Seven Things Children Need,* John Drescher says, "Acceptance means respecting a child's feelings and his personality while letting him know that wrong behavior is unacceptable. Acceptance means that parents like the child all the time, regardless of his or her acts or ideas." Heidi needed to feel secure in our love before she was free to reach out and welcome Kristin into her world.

Kristin herself played a major role in Heidi's eventual acceptance of her. The force of her personality attracted Heidi. And Heidi was delighted when Kristin became more than the baby sleeping in the corner and began to smile, coo, and sit. Then finally she changed into a walking, talking playmate of Heidi's.

In the years since our initial encounter with sibling rivalry, I have done a great deal of reflecting on how parents can assist one child in learning to accept another. Drawing on the failures and strengths of our own experience, these few observations have emerged:

1. *It is not possible to fully prepare a very young child for the birth of a new baby.* Although it is helpful to include the older child in preparations, the full implication cannot be explained verbally but must be experienced by the child. The parent cannot remove the pain but must help the child feel secure while working through feelings.

2. *Children respond best to a matter-of-fact approach.* Telling the older child of the expected baby too far in advance over-emphasizes the future event, making it loom too large and threatening. A month or two of talk about the expected arrival is sufficient.

3. *Undue attention does not foster security in a child.* Our excessive attention to Heidi during her first two years of life complicated her struggle to relinquish her position as star performer. No child is equipped to handle the power of being in the spotlight, and a violent reaction can be expected when another actor steps onto the stage.

4. *Viewing marriage as primary keeps all family relationships in perspective.* It was easier to be supportive of the children after John and I had reestablished our emotional ties by reserving time for each other. The children survived well in the care of a sitter and even benefited from the spaces we planned in our togetherness.

5. *A child should not be conned out of his feelings but should be allowed to express them in acceptable ways.* We allowed Heidi to drink her juice from a bottle, again, at her request. Holding her during a temper tantrum, in silence, seemed to help dissipate her anger. When she became too aggressive, she was sent to her room until she was calm.

6. *Parents need to serve as guides in producing the behavior they desire from their children.* We erred in becoming angry when Heidi was disruptive. She only became more hostile. When we were able to see beyond how she was making us feel to how she was feeling, we were more gentle and loving, and she in turn stopped biting and hitting Kristin.

7. *It is helpful for parents to acknowledge their mistakes and ask for forgiveness.* Our children have much to teach us about forgiveness. They give it readily and hold no grudges. We also need to learn to pardon ourselves when we are imperfect.

8. *New parents need the help and support of friends and relatives.* Most cultures ease a young mother into her new role of motherhood by providing a person or persons to share her workload. But our society places such a premium on independence that a young couple is often isolated with a task too large for them to handle. Although we hired some household help, we were thankful for friends and relatives who offered love and understanding by bringing food, baby-sitting, sending letters, giving gifts, and listening.

9. *Cultivation of the spirit when demands are many is time well-spent.* It was helpful to be reminded that we were not in this business of parenting alone. Nor were our problems unique. Sibling rivalry dates back to early human history—to the story of Cain and Abel. Our responsibilities and the guidance available came into focus as we reflected upon God's plan for Christian parents. I particularly appreciated the book *Meditations for the New Mother* (Herald Press) by Helen Good Brenneman.

10. *Minimal intervention by parents in disputes is preferable.* Children are remarkably adept at settling their own differences, relieving the parent from pointing an accusing finger. As our daughters became more equal in bargaining ability, they developed skills of compromise. To decide who would leave the bathtub first or who would get the blue cup we invented a game called "Apples and Pears." I would choose one fruit, and the child who guessed correctly had her choice in

each situation. Sometimes when they had been fighting, each child was placed on a chair for five minutes, and a timer was set. By the time the buzzer rang, they had forgotten what caused their conflict and resumed play peacefully.

Although competition between our daughters still surfaces, it is no longer the dominant theme of their relationship. Fortunately, positive feelings can exist alongside negative ones, and it is gratifying to watch our daughters becoming bound together as they grow and share experiences. It is a long road from the bondage of jealousy to the freedom of genuine love, but when I see Heidi and Kristin laughing together and enjoying each other's company, I know it has been a journey worth taking.

3

Jean Lersch When Your Child
Begs and Whines

Dinner is over. You've mixed, cooked, dished, carried, and passed the food for your backyard barbecue. The children have gobbled their hot dogs, baked beans, potato salad, and Jello dessert. They've dashed for the swing set and the sandbox tire.

You're finally enjoying peace and freedom from demands. For the moment your chores are done, and you can relax with a cup of coffee while you chat with your neighbor. You take a deep breath and begin to unwind as you exchange weather commentary and other neutral topics.

But the momentary peace is shattered with an ever-increasing crescendo of cries, whines, and clamor for attention:

"Look, Mommy!"

"Watch me go down the slide, Mommy."

"Mommy, he pushed me."

"Joey won't let me play with the ball, Mommy."

"Push me on the swing, Mommy."

"Can I go across the street, Mommy?"

Jean Lersch is a team member of Brethren House Ministries, St. Petersburg, Florida, which conducts learning fairs and publishes materials for church school teachers throughout the country. Jean and her husband Phil have two grown children—John, a high school science teacher; and Susan, a college student preparing for speech therapy.

Why can't your children allow you a quiet conversation with friends? You've dealt with demands all day, either at home or at work. You want a chance to unwind and relax. Yet your youngsters' incessant demands in front of guests embarrass you and preclude any adult conversation.

But why should your stomach knot as you try to remain serene in this conflict? If you're a conscientious Christian parent, shouldn't you willingly set aside your own desires for those of your children?

Not necessarily. Constantly ignoring your own needs and catering to your children's begging may not be good for you or them. This response may merely delay repercussions that could later vent themselves when you're off guard.

It's true that children need attention and approval from their parents. But don't adults also need to be heard? In your backyard barbecue scene, both children and adults have basic needs. Listen closely to the pleas and boasts of children, and you may discover the same message adults cloak in their conversation.

Children say, "Look at me! See what I can do!" Or they may say, "I did it first! I was here first!"

Adults use the same themes but more subtly. They imply by their remarks, "Listen to me. Hear what I did." Or they might hide the meaning behind other words but mean, "I've done that before. If you think that's phenomenal, listen to my experience."

If we examine the messages of both children and adults both seem to be expressing the same human need: "I want to be valued. I want to be assured of a place."

To sort out these needs and bring some harmony in times like the backyard barbecue you may need first of all to get to the root of the problem. Then plan to invest time and energy to meet all your family's basic needs.

1. *Provide the approval children crave.* If your busy schedule, even church work, always prompts you to push children aside and refuse to notice them, their demands will merely increase. Affirm them when they show something they've done. Respond to their offerings; enjoy them. Allow yourself time for delight in what they bring. Try to give at least four times as much approval as censure.

"I like the colors in your picture. I see the dog you drew. Would you like to tell me more about it?"

If this becomes your consistent response when John brings you one of his trophies, he will more likely accept your later request: "John, dad and mom would like to talk with our guest now. Will you please let us do that?"

2. *Provide the assurance children crave.* Often children nag their parents because they don't know what will happen. So they don't feel safe.

"Jeff, your mom and I will practice the song one more time and then you'll go home," I told the four-year-old. He had increased his whines for attention as his mother and I tried to rehearse. Both of us had been distracted, yet we were trying to overlook his nagging. After I had assured Jeff by explaining what would happen, he was content to wait "one more time" as he played with his toys.

When children know what will happen and what they may do, they feel safe. If they also believe they can gain recognition and approval for their efforts, they'll allow their parents time occasionally for personal pursuits.

3. *Clarify your values; then act on them.* Which do you want: a dwelling that qualifies for the cover of *House Beautiful* or children who feel approved and secure? If the perfect house arrangement were your desire, you would spend all your time

and energy cleaning, refinishing, and buying just the right accessories.

If emotionally healthy children are what you truly want, then allow time every day to listen to the messages they send. Provide a place where each child can play without fear of reprimand for making a mess.

Even cleaning up messes can be enhanced by labeled storage boxes for categorizing. "Let's keep all of the blue toys in the blue box, then the red ones can go in here." This might appeal more to children than the command, "Clean up your toys!"

Not only does this become a game. It also enhances learning. And if nurturing children is your goal, time spent with children planning and implementing such activities will also help them feel secure.

Which do you want: gourmet meals or children who are content? If the temperature and flavor of the food is your primary goal, you must say no to any requests that would interrupt timing of meal preparation. And television will help as you can direct the children to that "teacher" to insure your superb menus. But wait a minute. How soon will the ingesting of that food be over? And how soon will those children be grown and gone?

If investing time in your children while they are with you is your goal, plan simpler meal preparation that allows time for Dr. Seuss or some other childhood fantasy as the potatoes cook. The color and magic of children's stories bring more than entertainment for the children. Adults too can enjoy their whimsy. And shared enjoyment is a good base for secure children.

Sometimes parents need to remind themselves of their priorities. Why let advertisers or others choose what is important? You decide, then act.

4. *Identify and develop personal gifts.* No longer is it necessary to grind flour, card wool, milk cows, or wash clothes by hand. Some of us rarely iron. Often there is time free from duties. What do you want to do? What gives you satisfaction? Whom do you most admire? What is their contribution? Answers to these questions provide clues to the gifts you possess.

If in the time freed by modern conveniences you nurture these gifts, you may find yourself more willing and able to attend to your children's needs. If you are developing a skill that allows expression of your personality, you may not need to talk so much about your experiences.

But if you do only what you think others expect, you will crave compensation that may rob you and your children of the time you all need for satisfaction and affirmation.

5. *Take time for rest and recreation.* A walk in the park, a bike ride, listening to music, reading a book, attending a play or an athletic event will help remove you from your routines long enough for refreshment. Then you'll be ready again to attend to the needs of those within your "ministry."

The ultimate re-creation might be a directed weekend silent retreat where all of your attention is focused on God's priorities. And you will sense, after that focus, both your value and your security.

So conflict at the backyard barbecue need not upset your family's or your equilibrium. What you do at that moment to restore peace may not be nearly as important as your commitment to some long-range remedy. If you plan to provide daily the approval and assurance your children need, clarify and act on your personal values, identify and develop your gifts, and reserve time for personal rest and recreation, you will not only be able to cope with your family; you will also be able to enjoy them.

4

Neta Jackson

When Your Child Is Left Behind

Rachel bounced into her bed, "Bucky the Blanket" securely in hand. "What do you want to tell me?" she asked.

It was bedtime, but she knew something was up. Both Mommy and Daddy were there, and Daddy had a brand-new calendar in his hand. The three of us sat down on the bed together, and Daddy opened the calendar to August. He and I looked at each other over Rachel's head, both thinking: "This is it—it's time to tell her. How will she take it?"

Daddy cleared his throat. "Mommy and I have something special to tell you. We're going to take a trip far away—just Mommy and Daddy. And we're going to be gone two whole weeks, this many days." He drew a bright red line around the two weeks with a fat marker. "Let's count how many days that is. . . ."

We had known for several months about this trip, but we had decided to wait to tell our three-and-one-half-year-old daughter until two weeks before. It hadn't been an easy decision to make. My husband and I had been invited to participate in a conference on church renewal in Sweden. Our

Neta Jackson and her husband, Dave, parents of Julian and Rachel, are members of Reba Place Church, Evanston, Illinois. Between them they have written 20 books and study courses on such topics as church community, marriage and family, Christian relationships, and peacemaking.

church was enthusiastic about the idea, and Dave was certain it should be both or neither of us.

But the big question for us was: What about leaving our children for two weeks? Was our little girl too young? Would our absence be too hard for them? The longest we'd both been away from Rachel was a weekend. Two weeks was a different story!

We consulted a number of people in the church who knew our family well and had lots of experience with children. No one took lightly the problems often caused by parent-child separations. Basically, the counsel was: Rachel is a very verbal, well-adjusted little girl. If you prepare her properly and make good arrangements for the time you are away, she is old enough now to understand what's happening and not feel abandoned.

But what did it mean to "prepare her properly"? I talked with a number of people who had had to leave young children for various reasons (a stay in the hospital, a business trip, a family emergency). Here are some of the suggestions which proved helpful to us:

1. *Don't tell a little one too soon—or too late.* Our ten-year-old son, Julian, knew about the trip all along, but we waited until two weeks before to tell Rachel. This proved to be a good amount of time for her to get used to the idea. But it was not so far ahead that the concept of time was lost altogether.

2. *Use visual aids—especially a calendar—to help the child understand what's going to happen.* For both children we outlined the "days away" in bright colors on their own calendar. For Julian, we wrote on various days what he would be doing and where we would be. For Rachel, we bought little animal stickers, and every night as part of her bedtime routine she

stuck a sticker on the day just finished and then counted "how many more days till Mommy and Daddy leave on their trip." During the time we were gone, she stuck on a sticker and counted "how many days till Mommy and Daddy get back."

Other visual aids which could have been used: a picture of how the parents are going to travel (car, plane, train, boat) so the child can imagine what's happening; a picture or poster of the place the parents will be. Parents can tape these on the wall so the child can look at them before and during the absence. Dave used Richard Scarry's book about different modes of travel as a fun way to talk with Rachel about our trip.

3. *Use often the expression, "When Mommy and Daddy get back...."* One of the major problems for a small child in separations from the parents is fear of abandonment. Frequent and matter-of-fact references to being back together again will be reassuring to a child.

If possible, parents should point out events that will happen after the time apart to help the child look beyond the separation. We were able to say, "When Mommy and Daddy get back from their trip, Grandma and Grandpa are going to come, and we're all going to go camping—won't that be fun?" (We wrote this in on the calendar as well.)

4. *Decide which context will be easiest on your child during your absence.* For our oldest, a visit to two different sets of cousins seemed a perfect solution. For our youngest, however, we felt keeping to her normal routine in familiar surroundings would be the most secure thing for her.

We had the advantage of knowing a single woman from our church who had already lived with us, who often took care of the kids and knew their routine well. So Rachel stayed home with Denise, went to summer nursery school just like always, played with her friends, and slept in her own bed. Someone took care of her like "one of the family." Not many parents would have such an ideal solution—but it seems most important for a small child to be taken care of by someone he or she knows well.

5. *Make the time apart special for the child, too.* The visit to cousins was in itself special for Julian. But for our stay-at-home child, we planned a few special things she could look forward to during our absence: lunch at a friend's house, a trip to the zoo with Denise, new dimes in the piggy bank for a visit to the ice-cream store. "Special" doesn't have to mean elaborate or expensive—just something to look forward to.

We also left surprises: a stick of gum in an envelope, with "Love from Daddy" on it; a new comic book hidden in Julian's suitcase. Discovered after we were gone, these messages continued to say, "We love you and are thinking about you."

6. *Leave a picture of yourself for the child to keep close by.* When we got our passport pictures, Dave decided to use the extra sets for the kids. He put the pictures back to back and laminated them in one of those machines that do driver's licenses. He gave one set to Julian to carry in his pocket. With the other set he made a "necklace" for Rachel, punching a hole in the corner, fixing a metal eyelet into it, and stringing it onto an old chain. She was proud of her necklace and wore it to nursery school, giving her many opportunities to explain, "My mommy and daddy are on a trip, and these are my pictures."

7. *Make a tape recording of your voice for the child to listen to.* When Rachel's nursery school teacher suggested this to me, I thought it sounded a bit "much." But it turned out to be one

of the most important things we did. Part of Rachel's bedtime routine is for Daddy or Mommy to sing a couple songs to her. So we decided to continue that during the time we were away—on tape! We recorded 14 nights' worth of songs, with good-night kisses and little comments like, "Mommy and Daddy are traveling on an airplane tonight—maybe you can pray for us." Or, "Only three more nights and Mommy and Daddy will be back. We can't wait!"

Denise reported that the nights Julian spent at home "between cousins," he always came and listened to the tape, too. Afterward, he took the tape recorder and played all the ones he'd missed!

8. *Leave medical release forms for all adults who will have responsibility for your children.* We wrote ours something like this: "We hereby give permission for Betty or Bill Brown, relatives, to act in our behalf for our son, Julian Jackson, during our absence from the country, (dates), including emergency medical care should this be necessary." We had to do three for Julian and one for Rachel to cover all the adults who would be responsible for them at one time or another. We then signed these, had them *notarized,* and gave them to each adult as a legal document.

9. *Bring home a gift—and leave one too.* Gift-bringing after every little absence isn't a common practice in our family. But this was one time when it seemed especially important. The promise of a "little doll in native costume" for Rachel and "a Swedish souvenir" for Julian gave them something to look forward to. But at the airport the night we left we also gave Rachel an inexpensive doll in a "fairy godmother" dress and a new "micronaut" man for Julian to play with while we were gone. And by the way their eyes sparkled, even as we hugged

and kissed and waved good-bye, we knew we had communicated that this time was special for them, too.

From all we can tell, both kids weathered two weeks without Mom and Dad in good spirits. Oh, yes, there were lonely, fussy, and homesick days. And even though I expected Rachel to react with some negative behavior when we got back (either clinging to me or ignoring me), it just didn't happen.

This experience with a major separation taught us a few things to help with minor separations, too. Now when Daddy has to go away for a weekend, we mark it on the calendar and "count the days." We talk about what he's doing and pray for him often. When he gets back, we do something special, like play family games past bedtime!

We've also learned to keep pictures of grandparents and other relatives in the children's rooms and to talk about them and include them in nighttime prayers. This helps keep the relationship alive even though thousands of miles separate us.

Children notice. "I'm being thought of, too. I'm included." Little ones, especially, who don't verbalize as well as older children, need special help processing various changes in their family life. But the time and care are worth the results of the security and love which they feel.

5

Fern Clemmer When Your Child
Loses a Pet

After eager anticipation and much waiting, Valerie finally
had her pet—a yellow-striped kitten named Tiger. The months
passed, and I watched the kitten become a cat and the child's
fondness grow, trying to ignore the possibility that someday
our family might need to deal with the pet's death—we lived
near a very busy street.

One bright, cloudless morning in March, nine months after
the kitten came to us, my vague fear became stark reality. Our
neighbor's 7:00 a.m. phone call informed us that Tiger had
been killed in the early morning traffic. Suddenly my husband,
Dennis, and I faced the difficult task of dealing with the death
of our child's pet. We proceeded through five stages.

1. *We had to tell Valerie.* Sadly we drew already awakened
Valerie into our bed. As we reluctantly shared the unhappy
news with her, we saw her seven-year-old brightness fade
quickly into darkened grief. She sobbed brokenheartedly in
our arms. Our hearts were crying too, and we told her so, for
she wasn't the only one fond of the pet.

Fern Clemmer, Lancaster, Pennsylvania, and her husband Dennis are the parents of
Valerie and Tasha. Fern is director of information services at Lancaster Mennonite
High School.

2. *We helped Valerie face the reality of her pet's death.* By the time Valerie was dressed for school (she decided, despite reddened eyes and a heavy heart, that she would go to school), I had removed the pet from the street, straightened his twisted body, and placed him in his cushioned box on the back porch. Then Dennis and I led her to see, for herself, that Tiger was indeed gone forever. We cried together as Valerie stooped to stroke his soft fur, her young face turning sharply and agonizingly away when she saw the blood under his head. I was thankful Dennis and I had read and learned about this difficult, but important part of the grief process—seeing the reality of the death, thereby making it possible to move on toward the acceptance of it. It's tempting to hurry through or eliminate this phase, hoping to protect the child from overwhelming pain. Instead, this could interfere with the child's acceptance.

3. *We all discussed how, when, and where we would bury Tiger.* Since Dennis needed to leave for work soon and could not return until after dark, it was decided I would dig the grave beside one of our trees, and after school Valerie, four-year-old Tasha, friend Cindy, and I would bury our pet. While talking about these plans and how we would miss our feline friend's scratching at the door or bringing a trophy mouse home to show off, Valerie was further able to verbalize her feelings about her sudden loss.

4. *We buried our pet.* By 3:30, I had an adequate grave prepared beside the young maple in our yard. After several of Valerie's friends had come in to see Tiger and last good-byes were said, I placed Tiger in a pillowcase and carried him outside, the children following. When I had laid him in the grave, which was lined with his cushion, the children covered him

with the fresh dirt; I replaced the sod. Watching the children push the short stems of pussy willows (we were fortunate to have such an appropriate flower) into the soft ground around the grave, I noticed much of Valerie's heaviness had lifted. Involving her in the burial of her pet provided her with a satisfying way to express her sorrow.

5. *We continued to listen to and talk with Valerie about her loss.* Whenever Valerie needed to talk about her pet—the good memories, his death, her missing him—Dennis and I were ready to listen. This, of course, was true from the day the pet died as well as later. One day I overheard Valerie and her friend discussing the fact that Tiger was in heaven. I didn't confirm or refute this. After all, I don't know everything about heaven either. When Valerie is ready to learn more about the afterlife, we will search for the answers together.

Although the death of a family member or friend has a much more profound effect than the death of a pet, some of the feelings are the same. So, in dealing intelligently and sensitively with Tiger's death, I'm hoping we have helped prepare Valerie for other death experiences she will need to face.

6

Marlene Kropf When Your Child
Misbehaves
in Church

Normally I'm not a violent person. I'm your usual peace-loving person, a gentle soul who cringes at harsh words or fist-icuffs, let alone violence or killing. Nevertheless, I've felt the urge to kill all too often during a certain hour on Sunday morning.

Seated with my children in a worship service, I've wished I could bang their heads together, wallop them with a paddle, or at least deliver a good sound pinch.

On Sundays, we sit near the front of the meeting room so all of us can see and hear better. It also makes it more convenient for songleader dad to slip in beside us when he's finished with his duties. But that front and center position also makes it easy for everybody in the congregation to see how well our children misbehave.

One day I came to the unpleasant realization that I felt more anger and hostility toward our children in a one-hour worship service than I had felt in the whole week before. Something was obviously wrong. How could our otherwise adequately well-behaved children be so awful in church?

Marlene Kropf, Elkhart, Indiana, and her husband Stan are parents of Jeremy and Heather. Formerly from Portland, Oregon, Marlene taught English in public high schools for 11 years. Presently she works for Mennonite Board of Congregational Ministries and is a student at Associated Mennonite Biblical Seminaries.

First, I looked at myself. Why all the anger? Sunday morning worship has always been a special time for me. I love the singing, the praying, the sharing, the preaching. My oasis of spiritual refreshment was being threatened by our children's antics—and I was responding with normal frustration.

When I looked a little deeper, I saw that I was also humiliated and embarrassed by our children's misbehavior. After all, I like others to think I'm a capable parent. I teach Sunday school classes on child nurture and write an occasional article about children. I'm supposed to know a little something about kids. But there they were—big as life—kicking each other, pouting, refusing to stand when the congregation stood, whimpering, talking out loud, doing all the unruly things they could think of.

With that information about my own motives, I could proceed. As for pride, I'd just have to swallow it. But I thought twice about my enjoyment of worship. I decided I deserved that pleasure and would just have to get it for myself somehow. At least one family in our congregation simply leaves and goes home before the worship service begins rather than force their children to sit through a frustrating hour. But I need worship too much to do that, and I want my children to get at least minimal benefit from being in church.

Now my thoughts turned to our children. Our congregation provides children's church once a month during the worship service for school-age children, but the rest of the time it's up to parents to keep their children as happy as possible in a service that is obviously geared for adults. So what do we do with them when they misbehave?

Well, one old-fashioned solution is to take children out of church and spank them soundly when their behavior gets too bad. In desperation, we have tried that remedy several times. The trouble with that solution is that children spend all the prespanking time annoying and distracting everyone within earshot and spoiling their worship experience. Besides, we've never been convinced that spanking teaches good behavior anyway. We finally came up with four principles for surviving with kids in church.

1. *The first and simplest principle is to divide and conquer.* Children are never permitted to sit together but always have a parent positioned inbetween (heaven help the parents who have more than three children). It's much harder to misbehave alone than with an accomplice.

2. *The second principle is to foresee the obvious difficulties.* Our children make obligatory trips to the bathroom and drinking fountain just prior to the worship service. If that fails and ten minutes into the service our daughter still whispers, "I have to go to the bathroom," I say, "Wait a bit and see if you still need to go." Nine times out of ten she doesn't ask again.

3. *The third principle, and most significant for us, is to work on developing good behavior patterns* appropriate to the children's ages. For us, this meant discussing the problem of church behavior with our children, talking about our frustration and embarrassment, and deciding together on a course of action.

We made a behavior modification chart on which we kept a record of their weekly responses. We concentrated on just a few items at a time and reviewed them each Sunday morning at breakfast. During one month our eight-year-old's assignment was (1) to be pleasant in church (no angry scowls or nudges); (2) to try singing all the songs with the congregation; and (3) to listen to at least ten minutes of the sermon. Our five-year-old wasn't required to listen to the sermon (that happened when she turned six), but she was asked to sit and stand as the congregation did and not leave the sanctuary to go to the bathroom.

Another behavior we worked on was for our children (and us, too) to be able to tell at least one thing they had heard in the sermon. At first we were amazed to discover that next-to-nothing penetrates a child's mind from a sermon. But we did see improvement, and after several months, our children could begin to identify the theme of a sermon. More often they remembered the stories or some informal remark.

4. *The fourth and final principle is to prepare for the inevitable.* I nearly always slip a couple sheets of paper and some pencils and crayons into my purse before I leave for church. I make sure that our son takes along a book to read. When the children have lasted as long as they can, they must have something quiet to do. And when it comes to quiet activities, I've found a more successful approach than simply saying to a child, "Well, draw something." Instead, I draw a squiggly line or a geometric shape on a paper and tell the child, "Now, complete the picture." That little bit of a suggestion prevents the refrain, "I can't think of anything to draw."

To maintain adequate church behavior is our goal for our children at present, but in the long run we hope to lay a foundation for the development of worshipful attitudes and the ability to respond to God. As my need to impress other people decreases and our children's good church behavior increases, I'm feeling less and less angry on Sunday mornings. In fact, I've discovered that the worship hour is a good time for being close to our children. We seldom sit side by side for an hour during the week. A church bench is a great place for touching them with affection—and that's a whole lot more fun than the urge to kill.

7

Mary Leatherman When Your Child
Goes to the Hospital

When she was three and a half, our daughter, Bonnie, was scheduled for her third eye surgery. By the time she arrived at the hospital, her roommate, Michele, was already in her hospital gown. Michele, also three and a half, was to have eye surgery by the same doctor, but this was her first hospital experience.

The same was true for Michele's parents, who had only been inside a hospital when she was born. They were extremely anxious as they took turns leaving the room for cigarettes and coffee. Michele did a good job reflecting their anxieties as she demanded more toys from the playroom, wanted to be held, did not want to be held—in short, spending only a short time at any one thing.

She soon attached herself to Bonnie, completely ignoring her parents. Bonnie had found the "surprise" she knew to expect packed in her suitcase, and now both girls played with the "stick 'em" book and the music box. Before the hour was up, I had them both on my lap, listening to the adventures of Pinocchio. Michele's parents were out pacing the hall.

Mary Leatherman, and her husband Bill, Doylestown, Pennsylvania, parent five adopted children. A part-time R.N. on the maternity floor at the local hospital, Mary enjoys cooking, baking, knitting, sewing, and reading to the children.

By the time the nurse came to announce time for the girls to get into bed for the "bee-stings," Michele had calmed down and Bonnie had all but forgotten that she wasn't at home. But the shots produced a whole new bag of tricks from Michele's parents: "It won't hurt." "We won't leave you." By the time she was wheeled out for surgery they were saying, "You're just going out in the hall."

By three o'clock that afternoon, the two little girls were returned to their room. When Bonnie woke up enough to realize where she was, just as she had the other two times, she calmly touched her patch and said, "That's my eye patch. Is it blue again, like the last one?" She soon asked for a drink and then sat up to color, even though one arm was taped to an armboard and the IV was still running.

But no one had thought to tell Michele about waking up to eye patches and a needle in her arm. So she lay in the next bed with her arms tied down because she had already pulled off one of her eye patches and dislodged the IV needle.

I admitted to Michele's parents that my having been a pediatric nurse for two years did help me tremendously with Bonnie. "And different children react differently to a strange hospital environment and the new sometimes painful things they experience," I said. I would have liked to have told them that children soon reflect the attitudes and feelings of their parents about new situations. And that one of the best ways to help a child while in the hospital is to prepare him for the experience beforehand.

How is this done?

Most surgeons now provide written detailed instructions about a hospitalization including what can be expected to take place. They tell a child if there will be a cast, bandage, or eye patch after surgery and a parent can put a close resemblance of one on the child, explaining that he will be sound asleep when the doctor "fixes" him up only to wake up and find the bandage already done.

Another way to prepare a child is to "play" some of the other things he might experience: taking a temperature, eating dinner off a tray, sitting in bed, sponge bath from a basin while in bed. If the child will need blood tests, a parent can tell him it will hurt for a moment, but praise him about how brave he usually is; and "it hurts less if you hold very still and cooperate." Sometimes games can be made up. The child counts to 10 as fast as he can to see who gets done first. Injections become "bee-stings" as the child does the "buzzing."

Let the child help pack the suitcase with his favorite pajamas, robe, and slippers. Put in the stuffed animal, toy, or special pillow he usually sleeps with. Let him choose a favorite familiar toy suitable for a hospital, and you supply a few small gaily wrapped surprises that will increase the anticipation of unpacking. Include some "quiet" things to do: paper dolls, stick-'em books, short story books, or new crayons and a new coloring book. Even the smallest boy likes a new matchbox racing car or a little red tractor to "drive" around the crib.

Should you as a parent plan to stay with your child while he is in the hospital?

When Angie needed to go to the hospital for heart surgery six years ago, her mother asked the pediatric nurse, "Do you think I should plan to stay with her all the time or just visit each day?" "Oh, children adjust quickly to their new surroundings after the mother is out of sight," the nurse explained. "In fact, most children cooperate better without their mothers." But Angie's mother decided she would reserve a cot and stay at the hospital anyway. The surgery went well, and Angie's recuperation was so rapid she was hospitalized only half the time estimated by the surgeon.

Not many years ago we were on the tail end of a twentieth-century pediatrics more interested in children medically than emotionally. Studies have now been completed on the emotional effects on hospitalized children who were separated from their parents in comparison to those who were not.

The findings were so astounding that most pediatricians now encourage one parent to stay with the child who needs to be hospitalized, especially those between the ages of three months and five years. A few have become so convinced of the value of "family-oriented" care they give special instructions to the parents and then make them responsible for such things as giving medications and changing dressings. Because of this, some have even lowered their rates!

Statistics are all well and good, but what about the parents who absolutely cannot stay with their child? One family had a "special" child at home who might have suffered more from the separation than the child in the hospital. Another child needed extensive studies followed by surgery which took a total of three weeks. For one parent to remain that long at the hospital with other children at home was impossible.

The answer for these families is adequate preparation. Many pediatric departments will even give a tour for the child and parents a few days before admission.

And there are other things parents can do.

Reinforce in the child's mind that he will never be completely alone, even when you are not there. There are other children either in the same room or just next door. There is always a nurse not far away. She will come if he rings a bell or calls, but sometimes it takes a few minutes.

Find out if that hospital has a candy striper or a volunteer "grandmother," who can look in on the child during the hours you will not be there. Large city hospitals have play therapists who see that each child who is well enough has supervised play either in his room or in the playroom.

The Christian parents have an added "comfort" to stay with their child. Prayers said by their friends in Sunday school and by their family give strength to children never to be forgotten, even as for adults. Little songs, with which even a small child is already familiar, take on greater meaning: "God takes care of me every day. . . . " "At nighttime when my prayers are said. . . . "

Be certain to tell your child in terms he can understand, exactly when you will be back. If he can't tell time, maybe he can understand "in time to feed you your lunch." If parting is very difficult, plan to leave a small wrapped "surprise" to be opened after you leave. For a child to cry is certainly normal. Reassure him that you understand his hurt and you will be back as quickly as possible. If the child is an infant, it may help to have the nurse or a roommate's mother stay by the crib for a few minutes.

Plan to be with your child when it hurts the most, like right after surgery. Reassure him frequently that he is doing just like you expected him to and will soon feel much better. Many children fear they are dying when they experience severe or unusual pain, such as in tonsillectomies.

Whether or not you can stay with your child during his hospitalization, and regardless of what he is hospitalized for, always be truthful and share as much information as possible. I've seen what happens to too many children who were completely unprepared and often lied to. One mother had told her young daughter they were going to the hospital just to see the new babies and then left her to have her tonsils removed!

Finally, there are many helpful books available from your public library about being hospitalized written for various age levels. Librarians will be glad to suggest the most current and useful titles. Or if you're willing to invest in books and magazines, try the most service-minded bookstore near you.

8

Roberta Mohr # When Your Child
Steals

I was six years old when I stole a shiny octagonal tin compact from an elderly neighbor's home. The powder was gone from the compact, but the tiny mirror fascinated me. Perhaps it was the unusual shape. No one ever questioned me about taking it, but I felt terribly guilty. I couldn't even enjoy playing with it, so I hid it in the barn.

We all begin life with a natural desire to take what we want when we want it. As soon as two babies are old enough to snatch toys away from each other, they do it. Parents immediately insist the potential mugger return the toy. Children learn early that taking something from someone else, whether openly or in secret, is wrong. They learn to feel guilty and either to stop doing it or at least avoid being caught and punished.

But is the guilt a child feels over being caught taking a toy away from another child (or stealing a pack of gum in the supermarket) any different from the guilt a child feels over such things as wetting one's pants?

Roberta Mohr, Wadsworth, Ohio, and her husband Jim are parents of four grown children. After teaching college courses for five years, Roberta has chosen to return to her first love—small children—and now teaches kindergarten in the Wadsworth City Schools. A pastor's wife (First Mennonite, Wadsworth), Roberta is on the Board of Education and Publication of the Central District of her denomination.

To deal with such questions, Lawrence Kohlberg has developed a theory about the stages of moral development in a child. At the very first level, labeled *pre-conventional,* the child interprets moral situations only in terms of personal physical consequences. The child acts to meet his or her own desires and needs. The child seeks to avoid punishment or obtain rewards.

At this stage decisions are made without any understanding of morality. The guilt a child feels over stealing is no different from any other kind of guilt a parent imposes on a child through threat of punishment. The parent decides what acts are "bad," such as wetting the bed, running out in the street, or crayoning on the walls. Disobedience in any of these areas brings punishment. For the child, stealing is not yet seen as a greater sin than any of these other acts of disobedience.

The fact that stealing is morally wrong is too abstract a concept for a preschooler. But understanding that he or she will be punished for taking whatever does not belong to him or her is a very important first step in moral development. Returning the object to the owner is usually sufficient discipline. For effect, that needs to be done immediately, not the next week.

Some parents get overly upset when a young child has stolen something. Their initial reaction is "Not *my* child!" They're sure this is the first sign of juvenile delinquency.

Historically this has been the adult attitude. There was a time when children caught stealing were thrown in jail with hardened criminals. Stealing in the early years, however, simply means children are yielding to nature impulses which they must learn to control. They are not criminals, nor should they be considered sinners.

On the other hand, if a parent views the taking of a toy from a friend's home with a kids-will-be-kids attitude, this can also have dire consequences. The child took the toy car; the parent knew it and didn't make the child return it, so the child tries taking something else. It's an easy way to get new toys! It makes stealing a habit, and habits are hard to break. It also eliminates the feeling of guilt, something essential for moral development.

How do children move from this beginning level to the next stage of development? Kohlberg defines as *conventional* the next level, at which time a person interprets moral situations in a conforming way, first by wanting to please others and later by showing respect for authority and the social order.

A three-year-old named Sondra is being exposed to the conventional level every day by her parents. I watched her take a puzzle away from another child recently. When she saw me, she immediately returned the puzzle without my saying a word.

"I gave it back," Sondra said. "Are you proud of me? Does that make you happy? That makes my mommy proud of me. Mommy and Daddy are so happy when I be nice."

Sondra's running commentary on making everybody proud and happy doesn't mean she is already in the conventional stage. If I had not been watching, she may have gone ahead and taken the puzzle from the other child. I don't know how many inner controls she has developed, but at least Sondra is aware that her parents want her to act in certain acceptable, conforming ways.

After the conventional level comes the *post-conventional,* defined by Kohlberg as the time when an individual makes moral decisions out of respect and concern for the welfare of others. That sounds like Matthew 7:12—the golden rule!

As Christian adults we wish we could say this is where we are operating, but a closer look at our own motives reveals that we often make decisions on lower levels. Understanding ourselves will help us better understand our children. We know preschoolers are on the preconventional level, but we may not fully understand the level on which our teenagers operate.

Sometimes teenagers appear to be mature Christians operating at the conventional level when suddenly they shock parents and community alike by shoplifting. What motivates a bad decision like that?

The most common reason for a Christian teenager to steal is strong peer pressure. This can result from boredom. A group of teens with a day off from school and nothing to do enters a store just to look around. The game begins when one dares another to take something. They don't expect to be caught. They may not even consider it stealing because they're not taking anything valuable. If they're caught, they may be at a loss to explain "why" they did it.

There are many other motives for teenage stealing. Some youth attempt to "beat the system." Some stealing is a symptom of a much deeper problem, such as the need for money to purchase drugs. A few teenagers steal maliciously, deliberately taking objects with particular meaning for other people. Inability to find a job is another reason, although not so common a reason as one might think. Teenagers with money to spend are just as likely to steal as poorer teenagers.

In small towns store owners try to give local teenagers a break and let them off with a warning and a call to their parents. But teenage offenders who are serving sentences for stealing state that they wish someone would have dealt more harshly with them the first time they stole something. Getting off easy the first time gave them a false sense of security and encouraged them to do it again.

My son witnessed the arrest of a teenager recently in a local supermarket where he works. The manager has a "get tough" policy with shoplifters and called the police immediately.

"You should have seen that guy," my son said. "He was seventeen years old, a real big guy, and crying like a baby!" He had stolen a large chocolate candy bar in a Christmas wrapper, worth about $2.00.

In many cases, one arrest followed by probation in their parents' custody is enough to scare a teenager into being a law-abiding citizen. It depends on the support provided by family members, the amount of continuing pressure felt from the peer group, the teen's view of his own self-worth. Some teenagers and even younger children don't—or can't—stop stealing in spite of punishment.

What should parents do when they discover their child, at whatever age, is stealing?

Prayer definitely can change people, and parents should not neglect this important source of help. But God also works through psychiatrists who counsel with children who feel a compulsion to steal. Often family counseling is a good option, since many children steal to get attention. A counselor can help other family members to determine what, if any, behavior of theirs is contributing to a child's compulsion to steal.

Parents shouldn't wait until a child steals and then react with punishment. Parents should reward good behavior with hugs, smiles, and verbal praise as well as occasional treats. Sufficient attention must be given to acceptable behavior; thus disobedience is not a means for getting attention and punishment is needed less frequently.

Parents have an obligation to show by their example that they respect law and authority themselves. This is because it is their responsibility to help protect the rights of everyone in our society.

Most important of all, parents should work to develop a good self-concept in each child from birth. A child needs to understand how important he or she is to the family. The child who feels good about self and who loves his or her parents will want to please them.

A study by Purdue University researchers on teenage shoplifting revealed that assisting with family chores and joining in family financial decision-making, such as where to go on vacation or which car to buy, promoted attitudes which discouraged shoplifting. The basic feeling of being needed and contributing to the well-being of the family is essential for moral development.

9

Jane P. Moyer When Your Child
Worries Too Much

Several types of fears seem to be common to almost all small children. Child psychologists say the basic fear of small children is that of separation from the mother. Fear of sudden or loud noises seems to be present from birth, and even new infants display signs of fear when they feel as though they are falling. From the preschool years on, many children have a pronounced fear of the dark and of thunderstorms. Doctor and dentist visits and barbershop experiences provide a source of anxiety for many youngsters. One friend told me that her six-year-old sometimes worries, while traveling in the car with her parents, that they might get lost and be unable to find their way home. Another friend's four-year-old is afraid to flush the commode.

Although older children in the six-to-ten-year-old range seem outwardly to be quite independent and capable of handling more difficult situations, often they, too, experience worry when their family makes a move. They are afraid they will be unable to make new friends and are fearful of meeting a new teacher. Older children may still retain fear of water,

Jane P. Moyer, her husband Dave, and their daughter Diane live at Lancaster, Pennsylvania. They attend First Deaf Mennonite Church. Jane is the administrator of New Danville Mennonite School (kindergarten through grade 8).

especially if they have had a frightening experience with it in younger years. Increasing pressure from teachers and parents to perform well in school may cause some children to worry about failing. Peer pressure to conform to group norms may worry the child who finds it difficult or impossible to fit in.

Sometimes it is hard to know when a child is worrying about something. The aggressive child may become more aggressive, and the shyer child may become even more withdrawn. And sometimes the signals they send out are difficult to interpret. When our daughter was six, she became tense and hyperactive after we moved to a new community just prior to the beginning of school. It seemed that, suddenly, she was no longer able to cope. Normally quite sunny, she was easily frustrated and constantly burst into tears at the smallest provocation. I was growing exasperated until I began to listen. "I won't have any friends," she said. "I don't want to go to school. I wish we'd never moved to this old place." It is generally safe to assume that an abrupt change in a child's behavior is a sign that he or she may be worried about something which is more than the child can handle at the moment.

The causes of children's fears are not always easy to spot. One mother reported that she noticed her son washing his hands repeatedly. At the dinner table he was cautious about eating certain foods. It was only after questioning him that she realized he was afraid of being poisoned accidentally. Previously, he had swallowed aspirins and had to have his stomach pumped. Of course, his parents justifiably warned him quite thoroughly of the danger of eating pills. This experience left him with an acute anxiety about poisoning.

Some children become anxious when they experience the death of a close relative. After five-year-old Timmy's grandmother died, Timmy began crying each morning and refusing to go to kindergarten, which he had previously enjoyed.

Whenever his mother complained of something as minor as a headache, he became concerned. Several times he asked her if she was old. Upon the suggestion of his doctor, his mother talked to him about his grandmother's death even though she felt sure he had understood quite well at the time she died. To her surprise she found that Timmy was afraid that she might die, too. He feared that, if he went to kindergarten, she might die before he got home.

Since almost all fear is learned, one of its most frequent causes is the child's observation of the reaction of adults around him to frightening events. When four-year-old Shawn was in the barn watching his parents milk the cows, a severe summer thunderstorm developed. Lightning struck the metal pipes in the barn, and fire followed down the entire row of stanchions. Involuntarily, his parents screamed. For months afterward, Shawn was frightened of thunderstorms almost to the point of hysteria. However, if parents are able to react calmly to a stressful situation, this calmness is communicated to the child.

But even though parents may feel they are discussing something in a reasonable manner, anxiety may still be produced in the child. Since a child does not have access to all of the information that an adult does, perceptions of reality are often distorted. I remember being quite worried as a child that my parents would be unable to pay their bills. I listened with dread when my mother stood, pencil in hand, checking the calendar to see when the mortgage was due. I had heard somewhere that "people go to jail if they don't pay their bills." To me, my mother's rational concern about meeting a monthly obligation portended something much more fearful, especially if I had been told the day before that there was not enough money to buy candy.

Sometimes older children are responsible for producing

worry in the minds of smaller siblings or playmates. When my daughter began having nightmares about monsters and had to be reassured several times at bedtime that there were no monsters in the house, I began to wonder what started this sudden concern. Later I overheard an older neighbor girl relating wild tales of "bigfoot" and play-acting terrifying monster scenes.

The effect that frightening fairy tales and monster shows on the TV have on small children is an issue on which authorities in child-rearing do not agree. Some say that the scary world of rogues and witches provide an outlet for children to vent safely their bottled-up hostilities in a healthy fashion. Others say such overly horrifying tales should be avoided because they overstimulate the child and produce real anxiety. Most, however, would agree with Dr. Lee Salk, author of the bestseller, *What Every Child Would Like His Parents to Know;* that although it may be beneficial for a child vicariously to experience a release of aggressive feelings toward others, the child should certainly be able to "walk away" from that type of situation when it becomes more than he or she can handle. Parents need to be alert as to when this level is reached.

Although it is important to know why a child is bothered, it is not enough. What does a parent do to help a worried child? In talking to other mothers, I found that there are plenty of commonsense approaches. One grandmother stressed (I found later that she has considerable support from child psychologists) that it is important to check whether the worried child is in good physical health and if overly tired. Exhaustion and poor health can contribute to a child's tendency to worry.

The importance of preparing a child for a new situation by explaining and play-acting the situation before he or she actually encounters it should not be overlooked. When we realized our daughter's fear of attending a new school, we

took her to play on the school's playground equipment.
Several days before school began I took her to meet her new
teacher and to become oriented to her new classroom. Fortunately, one of her new classmates was there at the same time
and my daughter was able to start school a few days later with
the feeling that she had made at least one new friend already.
Within a week or two almost all of the symptoms of her previous anxiety had vanished completely.

Talking to a child about fears is a solution used by many
mothers. Laughing at fear or pointing out the utter ridiculous-
ness of it is never helpful. Children's fears are real and they
will probably react by clamming up and somehow feeling infe-
rior for having such unworthy feelings.

Allowing a child to verbalize fears helps lessen their impact.
Sometimes it helps for a youngster to hear parents relate
similar fears which they experienced when they were young. A
few years later, the child may be willing and even enjoy laughing at the very thing which worried him or her so much previously.

Another solution which several friends mentioned as being
particularly vital in a Christian home is to use the situation as
an opportunity to help the child experience a feeling of trust
and security in God's protection by teaching prayer about
whatever is bothering the child. When six-year-old Chris was
afraid that there would be a fire during the night and that her
family's house would burn down, her mother suggested that
she ask Jesus to keep the house from burning. It has become a
nightly ritual which provides a considerable amount of
comfort and security to Chris.

However, there are times when a child's anxiety reaches an
acute level and there is no simple solution. No amount of talking will convince a child who has an unreasoning fear or
phobia. Child psychologist Dr. K. E. Moyer writes in her

book, *You and Your Child,* that "re-conditioning" is the only truly effective measure.

Gradually reacquainting a child with the source of fear in pleasant circumstances over a period of time may cure the phobia. If a child is afraid of water, it is seldom successful to suddenly throw that child into the water in an attempt to force him or her to overcome fear. Instead, the child should be able to gradually replace unpleasant memories of water with pleasant associations.

At no point should the child be pushed further than he or she is willing to go. If force is used, panic will usually result, and the original fear will actually increase. It will take longer to go slowly, but eventually the child will conquer the fear.

It is good to remember, when considering the fears of one's child, that a certain amount of fear or worry is normal and to be expected. Every effort to provide a reasonably happy and secure home environment should be made. Actually a worried child needs much the same kind of support that an adult does.

We all need someone to whom we can confide our anxieties and from whom we can be assured of receiving warm acceptance and love in return. If the level of fear becomes unmanageable, this support must take the form of professional help. But for most children the passage of time and understanding adults who intelligently provide the necessary help are enough to help the child learn to cope with the fears and anxieties so common in life.

10

Mary Leatherman # When Your Child Wants to Play with Guns

"Guns! Cowboy guns! That's what I want for my birthday. That's what I really want. Nothing else—just guns." How often we heard that emphatic request as our son approached his fifth birthday.

My husband and I had always thought we'd just follow the rule both our parents had—no toy guns. After all, wasn't that the accepted stand for all good nonresistant Mennonite homes?

Yet we noticed that our children (including girls) found sticks with little resemblance to guns but with quite effective shooting abilities. Or Lego blocks and Tinker Toys took on the shapes of rifles and pistols very quickly. When visiting "guns-allowed" homes, guns were the first things our children pulled from the toy box.

What should we do? We discussed it with our friends who had children of similar ages and interests, wondering if it wouldn't be better to buy the toy guns and then use them as tools to teach against violence. Around that time, we read about a similar problem, and the author claimed that after toy

Mary Leatherman, and her husband Bill, Doylestown, Pennsylvania, parent five adopted children. A part-time R.N. on the maternity floor at the local hospital, Mary enjoys cooking, baking, knitting, sewing, and reading to the children.

guns did become allowed, they were soon discarded in favor of toys far more interesting.

So Dad purchased the memorable set of cowboy guns, complete with holster and hat. What an exciting birthday! Oh, Mike probably could have been convinced to be happy with something else, but the guns would still have been very much on his mind.

About that same time, our local newspaper carried two stories of tragedies that had happened with guns. The first involved a 16-year-old boy who came in from checking his traps, gun in hand. He'd been taught the proper use of a gun, but he *knew* that it wasn't loaded. As a trick on his 14-year-old sister, he sneaked up behind her, shouting, "Stick 'em up." The gun was loaded, and he killed his only sister.

The second incident involved a party for a football team in one of the player's homes. Sure of some exciting fun, the half-back pulled out a pistol, pointed it at his favorite teammate, and killed him instantly. He, too, *thought* the pistol was empty.

We discussed the horrors of those tragedies with our children. And we also made a rule: no pointing guns—not even in play—at people. Like their dad, who is a hunter, they too could use guns for rabbits, pheasants, and deer (or to keep the monsters away) but never to be pointed at people.

It took many reminders and much repeating, but eventually that rule made an impression. Once when it was openly violated, we put the guns on top of the refrigerator for a week. That was all it took to ingrain the seriousness of the rule. Recently, even little two-and-a-half-year-old brother, Doug, was overheard telling his still younger friend, "Don't shoot people, Kevin, just rabbits and pheasants." When the advice wasn't taken seriously, Doug came running and cried, "He shooted me," making me feel my efforts were paying off.

Then there were the games children played. One day a neighbor, Tim, was here playing, and suddenly the powder room became a trench. All the boys were the "goodies" with the "baddies" being imaginary but shooting down the boys every time they emerged from the "trench." I listened for a while but decided to let this one go since they weren't actually shooting at each other. The game continued with much running around and falling down, including sound effects.

When it was time for Tim to go home, the "war games" came to an abrupt halt. Earlier, both boys had left their lunch boxes on the back step after getting off the bus. They had stayed outside to play in the snow awhile, and Doug had joined them in their play. Without them realizing it, I had picked up Mike's lunch box and brought it inside. Now, as Tim was leaving, he picked up his lunch box, reminding Mike that his was missing. Mike somehow quickly deducted that his younger brother had carried it off and proceeded with, "If you took my lunch box out there in the deep snow, I'm going to kill you."

I was horrified! He had never said that before. Yes, I knew he loved his little brother and, no, he'd never actually do it. But I've always felt it was important for people to express as carefully as possible how they felt and what they meant, not just to spout off words to vent their frustrations. I got the feeling that the "war games" were still going on in his subconscious, so to kill the offender was the natural thing to do. I decided then there would be no more "war games" at our house.

A lot of publicity has been given to the damaging effect of TV on children and the violent shows available on prime time. For most children, it's got to be difficult to interpret why Mom and Dad react so emotionally to local shooting but sit and watch the same thing on TV with no show of emotion. At least, I've never seen anyone turn away with a "Oh, no!" or

"That's awful; I can't believe it!" while viewing Westerns, de-tectives, or lovers as they shoot at each other show after show.

"Movies" are a problem for young children to figure out when they appear so realistic. For this reason, a variety of games have become after-supper fun at our house and we turn on the TV only for specials. Saturday morning cartoons are still somewhat of a problem. We have narrowed it down to *Bugs Bunny, Roadrunner,* and the *Pink Panther,* but even in their seemingly harmless antics these have many violent un-dertones.

Killing is nothing new, and TV can only be blamed in con-text with other exposures our children have to violence. It is, after all, the parents' attitudes that are "caught" by the children.

As far back as records have been kept, people have killed each other intentionally. Even King Saul tried very hard to kill his own son's best friend, David, all because of a nasty rumor he heard about David's popularity versus his own. It was the chief priests and the scribes who schemed to kill Jesus when he interfered too much with their lifestyle. And still today, people take other people's lives because of jealousy, because of simple threats, or while playing games.

Are we being effective as we teach our children? We'd like to think we are. We feel it's worth a try to teach them that human life is very precious. And, in time, we trust they too will adopt the nonviolent way as the Christian way to live.

11

Vel Shearer When Your Child
Goes to School
for the First Time

For five—almost six—years our son had been in our care.
Of course, there were times of play with Diana next door and
interactions with other children. But now September was coming, and Jody would go to school for the first time. Suddenly it
hit me that more of his waking hours would be spent in that
classroom with some unknown teacher than with his parents. I
was frightened and just a bit anxious.

But Jody was eager for school to begin. The problem was
mine. Having been a schoolteacher, I knew it would be easy to
be critical of his teacher's techniques and abilities. In retrospect, I would probably have heard some anxieties on Jody's
part, too, had I listened more actively.

Our second son reminded me that children have concerns
for that first day of school. When Jay entered kindergarten, he
was still four; he would turn five in October. I had plenty of
questions about that. The teacher was eager to let Jay come.
She was confident it would work out. If not, he could stay
home or spend two years in kindergarten, she said.

With her confidence supporting me, I took Jay to a "visiting

Vel Shearer, Wilkes-Barre, Pennsylvania, and her husband John are the parents of
Jud, Jody, and Jay. Vel is a counselor/parenting specialist in a program for single
parents and homemakers at Luzerne County Community College. She also edits
Voice, a magazine for the women of the Mennonite Church.

65

day" for the prospective kindergarten children. It was spring. The regular class activities were happily proceeding, allowing the visiting children an opportunity to see what they would be doing next year in kindergarten. They were free to join in, when and where they wished.

I left Jay looking very quiet and sitting at a table. We visiting mothers were served coffee in the gymnasium during the hour the children visited. After thirty-five minutes, Mrs. Dipple and Jay appeared at the door.

"He says he wants to see you." Mrs. Dipple brought Jay to where I was sitting. He wasn't in tears. He just announced it was time to go home.

On the drive home, I inquired about what he'd done.

"I sat at the table."

"All the time?" I knew for sure now that my four-year-old was not ready for kindergarten.

"Ah-huh—then we had cookies."

"That must have been nice—but, Jay, why didn't you play with the toys and games? Mrs. Dipple said you could." We were home now and sitting at the kitchen table.

"Well, you see, Mom, I wanted to look things over and watch how they did things so I'd know."

What a boy! How could I help but hug him? He knew much better than I what he was needing to experience through that visit. Although it has been difficult, since then I have tried to tune into my child's feelings in any new experience.

In our family there have been several first days of school for our three sons. The first day in a new school in fourth grade in our experience has similar feelings to the first day of school when the child began his first year of formal education.

When we moved to Elkhart, Ind., our sons attended a large inner-city school. This was in contrast to a small country school which they had just left in Canada. On the first day of school, Jody, then in fourth grade and Jay, in second, announced that they were not going to have my husband, John, or me come with them.

I was dubious. Some inner feelings alerted me that they were perhaps expecting too much from this new situation. We asked questions but agreed to let them go. They had been preregistered so that would not be a problem. I waited anxiously, part of me grateful that they felt secure enough to try that adventure, but praying that God would send some caring teacher to help them find their way.

At nine o'clock fourth-grader Jody came running in the back door of our apartment, crying and afraid. He hadn't been able to find his classroom.

"Oh, it's so big, Mom. I couldn't understand what they were saying. And I didn't know where to go."

He was obviously very frightened. He trembled as I held him to me. After another good cry I took him back to the school. The principal was understanding and showed us to Jody's classroom. He hesitated a moment at the door and then said, "Don't come in, Mom. I'll be okay."

Not seeing Jay anywhere, I assumed he'd found his way. But his first words on coming home were, "I had to cry today, Mom. Then a teacher found me and showed me where to go."

"That must have been scary."

"Yeah. Boy, is it a big school. But I know where my room is now."

For Jay it was settled. This was going to be his school. For Jody the struggle lasted several weeks. In the country school he had been one of the older children. The rule of thumb was that they helped the younger ones. In this school the sixth-graders "ruled the roost" and some of the children from insecure family situations bullied on the playground.

It was easy for me to say, "They need you as a

friend, Jody. Just be friendly." I was naive. That was not the language of the street. The rule of thumb for these children was to test the endurance of the new students.

We cried a lot together those days—and prayed. The assurance we sent Jody with each day was that we would always be there to help and that God was with him. We learned together that not everywhere is the world so serene and loving as school in rural Canada. We also concluded—without any persuading—that when Dad was through seminary and we would have to move to another school, on that first day Mom or Dad would go along.

Perhaps the first child in the family has the advantage in his first school experiences. He has not heard from older brothers about "the big kid who's beating up everybody" or about "the teacher who's yelling all the time."

Our third son had plenty of opportunity to hear these stories. It became obvious that sometimes he worried about his brothers while they were at school. One morning Jud was playing quietly in our living room. I heard him singing, "Kum Ba Yah."

"I like the song you're singing, Jud."

He looked up at me and said very seriously, "Do you know who I'm singing it for?"

I shook my head.

"I'm singing it for Jay at school today."

Jay had been having difficulty accepting his teacher expressing anger to his friends. She wasn't angry at him, but it was worrisome to Jay to have her yelling at his best buddies. Jud had heard Jay's struggle about it that morning. Often he said little when his brothers referred to stress situations at school. That should have been a clue for me that he was concerned. I have tried to decide whether Jud's struggle with his first day of school was due to his own lack of confidence or how much the stories he had heard from his brothers and the children in the neighborhood intimidated him.

During the first days of kindergarten it was a struggle for Jud to leave home. John and I would take turns walking with him and his best friend, Brian. Suddenly he would let go of our hand and say, "I can go by myself now" and he and Brian would go merrily on their way. As the days and weeks went by the distance we walked with him shortened. Soon we were walking only to the end of the backyard. Then a good-bye kiss at the door was sufficient. We had learned with this third child that our biggest task was to reassure him that we would be with him as much as he needed.

In Jud's kindergarten situation—and in his first days here in his current school—the bridge from home to school was built by his request for a note to tell the teacher about his struggle. On both occasions I wrote a simple note to the teacher, telling her that Jud was having difficulty coming to school and that he wanted me to write a note telling her about his problem. The teachers were both understanding.

Growing up happens and needs change. Fifth-grader Jay isn't about to have me tell the teacher about any stress he may be feeling. And seventh-grader Jody went to the new junior high school without Mom or Dad as escorts.

There are no simple answers and very few standard solutions on how to help a child through that first day of school or the first weeks in that new situation. Sometimes a visit to the new school or meeting a new teacher before the actual first day may ease anxiety. Or it may be helpful to have established a relationship with another kindergarten child before school begins. We discovered, though, that friends at home are not necessarily close friends at school.

Although a visit to the classroom and other attempts to ease the situation have helped, these encounters did not make much difference when the actual experience of being at school with the new teacher and classmates took place.

When coming to Wilkes-Barre, we chose to move in the summer, assuming the boys would have ample time to meet new friends and become familiar with the community. Although we knew children lived on our street, few were around in the summer. One day I suggested to our three that I help them meet two boys we'd seen across the street.

"No way!" was the three-toned chorus.

"Well, how are you going to make friends?"

"Look, Mom," Jody was the spokesman. "When school starts and its time to make friends, I'll make them. I have my way." And all of them did make friends, in their way.

We have discovered, sometimes through pain, that as parents we need to be honest about our feelings—to look at them, feel them, own them, so they will not get in the way of caring for our children. A standard rule for us has been to listen carefully to the spoken and unspoken messages about stress situations the children may be experiencing and then to reassure them that we will support them whatever may happen.

We have learned that each child's needs vary as to how that support should be given and how much we should communicate to the school. During elementary and high school days when school was the world of our sons for ten months of the year, six to seven hours each day, we choose to keep a keen ear to what was happening there.

So when your child starts school for the first time, the best advice we can give of our experience is to be there—both in body and in spirit.

12

Esther Groves When Your Child
Has a Learning
Disability

The only year Nathan began public school eagerly was kindergarten. I walked to school with him the first day: a handsome five-year-old with dark, curling hair, clear brown eyes, and the beautiful golden tan of some Peruvian Indian ancestor. He was proud to be going to school and did not hold my hand until we came up the sidewalk to the kindergarten door. Then he may have felt some of the apprehension, yet also trust, that he showed years before as our newly adopted seven-month-old son.

The kindergarten teacher was smiling. Nathan knew two other classmates, his cousin and a neighbor girl. He was now a grown-up schoolboy; everything would be all right. And for a short while it was, more or less.

But then. . . .

What a sinking he must sometimes have felt as he saw the others learning letters and numbers from a puzzling design of black lines and white spaces. How he must have tried at first, believing the teacher when she said that if he tried harder he could see what everyone else saw.

Esther Groves, Turpin, Oklahoma, and her husband Carlyle are the parents of Debra, Nathan, and Quentin. Esther works as area editor, news reporter, and feature writer for the *Southwest Daily Times,* Liberal, Kansas.

His image of himself must have been damaged as he began to be humiliated and wounded by others' misunderstanding. What bravery and courage it must have taken, every year from then on, to go back to that scene of failure day after day.

He began to dawdle on the way to school, sometimes arriving late. Still we did not suspect. Nathan could not tell us what was going wrong, and the teacher said nothing until the end of the year.

There were other signs, but we did not know how to read them. He saw colors differently than we did. He had such good large-muscle coordination that he rode a bicycle the first time he tried, but his poor eye-hand coordination made tying his shoelaces difficult. He was hyperactive, excitable, and impulsive and got into so many things that he reaped many spankings at home and trips to the neighbors to apologize for this and that. At church, while my husband, Carlyle, sat with the choir, I and the children sat in the balcony near the exit to accommodate Nathan's short attention span.

Confidence in ourselves as parents was deteriorating. Carlyle and I became more critical of each other's handling of Nathan. "Boys are harder to raise than girls," I thought, remembering our daughter's childhood, smooth even with childhood diseases and accidents.

At the end of the school year the teacher called us in. Our child did not know his letters and numbers, and a psychologist had suggested testing. The tests showed that Nathan had a perceptual disability caused by an impairment of his nervous system.

Years later, I learned that a child may be quite intelligent and still have such an impairment. Albert Einstein was considered slow as a child, Hans Christian Anderson had trouble learning to read, and Winston Churchill was at the bottom of his class in school. The eye or ear itself may be normal, yet the child sees or hears differently from others because the nervous system is not receiving/storing/sending messages in a standard way—unusual "wiring," you might say.

The psychologist could not tell us with certainty what caused this condition. Nowadays some say heredity may be involved because four times as many boys have it as girls, and it sometimes seems to run in families. Another theory is that if an expectant mother has an inadequate diet—and what could be easier, with our wide choice of junk foods—she may not have enough calcium, magnesium, and certain B vitamins. Then, if during her pregnancy she also experiences stress, this makes diet deficiencies surface so that the fetus does not develop as fully in certain ways, and she has one of "those" children: hard to cuddle, hyperactive, with learning disabilities. One government estimate claims that as high as 15 percent of the population has a severe learning disability.

In school, the learning disability shows up in basic skills: reading, writing, spelling, arithmetic, speaking, or listening. Nathan's perceptual difficulty made it hard for him to draw, to keep his place on the page when reading, to remember, to grasp concepts, to read clock time. Another child with different "wiring" might have different problems.

During Nathan's testing, the psychologist rolled up a sheet of paper, handed it to Nathan, and asked him to look through it. Nathan took it with his right hand and put it up to his left eye. Later the psychologist recommended an eye patch and eye exercise games to strengthen the weak right eye. I bought black cotton and elastic, made two "pirate patches," and put one on Nathan. Suddenly he was very quiet, couldn't cope, had to get out of the house. He and Carlyle went for a walk hand in hand.

"Daddy, I'm frightened."

"What's wrong, son?"

"The cars are upside down."

This was the first time we knew that one eye had been seeing upside down and backward. The eye patch and eye exercises corrected this but not, of course, the nerve impairment.

That fall Nathan returned to kindergarten, and we paid for a tutor who had him trace sandpaper letters and numbers with his fingers so that he would learn them by feel. She had him draw the symbols large—in the air, on the blackboard, on her back—so that he would learn them through movement. In turn she traced them on his back for him to guess. The more of his senses that were involved, the more he learned.

Tutoring helped, but grade school was still not fun. Nathan remembers from then and later: "The words were hard to figure out. Sometimes I couldn't figure them out. They sort of looked alike and ran together. I cried sometimes in school because it was hard. It still is."

A student placed at such a disadvantage may resort to smokescreen stratagems such as clowning in the classroom in order to keep his peers' approval. "What is the capital of Afghanistan?" "Albuquerque!" he said with a big smile to indicate that of course I really know, I'm just hamming it up.

In 1972, we went to Sierra Leone, West Africa, to work for two years in a literacy program. I ended up teaching Nathan and his younger brother, Quentin, at home, since Nate still needed one-to-one tutoring. At least, he didn't have to be compared with others in his grade, and he could progress at his own speed. We used rubber nut counters, Cuisenaire number sticks, standard texts, a word-family book—and didn't quit school until African schools let out the middle of July.

I recall one interesting thing: when Nathan read aloud he

preferred to sit close by me on the sofa, soaking up emotional support almost by osmosis. I know now he was pushing himself to his limits and needed all the support we could give. Then, change came once again.

Friends in Turpin, Oklahoma, offered Carlyle work there on our return from Africa. I was not all that interested in moving to a new community until a letter came describing the school's new special education program. By the end of the letter I was mentally moving to the panhandle so that Nathan could have professional help.

What this help meant was three daily special education classes in basics, designed not for the mentally retarded but for children with learning disabilities. Other subjects Nathan took with the rest of his class. Since he was accompanied by seven other boys in the special education classes, he no longer had continuous one-to-one attention and had to back up and learn to work more on his own. His progress was more solid now: learning was reinforced with special learning materials and equipment, and his comprehension was more thoroughly tested.

This was great as far as it went. The catch is that it goes only through eighth grade.

This year Nathan is an eighth-grader. Next year in all his classes he will have what he now has in only two: textbooks with too-small print in lines too close together, using too-difficult vocabulary to present too-abstract concepts in too much text. What then? Obviously the ideal is a high school special education program, but this means hiring another special education teacher and finding an empty room.

The one ray of light is the fairly new law that says schools must provide instruction at the student's level. How this is applied depends on each school and teacher. Parents may request a hearing if the school is not complying with the law.

Last year Nathan took civics with his class. Carlyle recorded textbook chapters on cassette tapes, and the special education teacher used them in classes when the student was supposed to listen to words and follow them with his eye at the same time. However we all concluded that giving too-difficult material twice isn't the same as giving it to the student on his level.

This year we're trying something else. For American history I summarize each chapter in a longish paragraph, underlining the new words a student needs to know. His test over the chapter is the same paragraph, now with blanks for him to fill in, administered at school. This Cloze technique is a method teachers can use when there are no easy-reading texts for a particular course. I learned about it at the last ACLD (Association for Children with Learning Disabilities) national convention. Ideally, the teacher does this, but if the teacher isn't interested I'll gladly offer my help.

There are still ups and downs. Nathan said: "One time I got in a fight. The boy called me some bad names and said I couldn't do any work very good, and that I was retarded, so that made me very sad."

He worries about the future: "When I couldn't learn anything I thought I was stupid and dumb, and I thought I couldn't make my way in life, I'd never have a car or anything, I'd always be poor when I grew up." We reassure him that he can do many things (drive on country roads, raise pigs, take complete care of the lawn) and that he is able to learn vocational skills. Every child needs to feel that he is good at *something.*

A person with self-confidence can learn to compensate. I once heard of a young man with a learning disability so severe that he will never read above a second-grade level. He is now straightening fenders and the like in a friend's body shop.

When asked how he expected to handle a bank account and checkbook (his mother does it for him now), he laughed and said, "Oh, I'll have my wife take care of that!"

That's the spirit.

Parents can teach their children "survival skills" for living in the world. Perhaps the chief rule is: *don't give up!* Remember Annie Sullivan, in the play *The Miracle Worker* as she tried again and again to teach words to blind and deaf Helen Keller, saying the biggest sin is giving up? If it takes a thousand repetitions to teach something, well then that's what it takes.

But what can parents do who have a child with a learning disability to help that child and make the most of the situation? The ideas which follow are not all mine. Some grow out of our experience as family; others come from workshops I've attended and from reading.

1. *Invest in educational toys and games.* Let the child see parents having fun putting different kinds of puzzles together and playing games. Hide birthday presents and play "You're hot/cold" as the child looks. Plan treasure hunts and scavenger hunts.

2. *Buy socks of all one color if color is a problem.* Make charts to show which pants and shirts go together.

3. *Make or buy a large cardboard clock face with movable hands and sixty-minute spaces around the edge, if telling time is a problem.* First practice identifying the hours; later on, half hours. Then the child learns about minutes, counting how many all together and how many between each number. Next practice counting by fives. A couple of minutes a day on time-telling is better than one too-long session that kills interest.

4. *Use rewards for behavior motivation:* an M & M or a penny when the child is young, perhaps an accumulation of "tickets" that can be exchanged for something special, like bowling, when the child is older.

Let the child use "crutches" like computers for arithmetic and digital watches for time-telling. What these do is give the child some badly needed self-confidence about being able to master a situation. Don't pressure or overload the child. Above all, be patient, especially when the child forgets things previously learned, or becomes upset and angry.

5. *Keep directions simple.* Remember that the child sees or hears things differently (even adults in a hurry have mistaken "laddies" for "ladies"). Present new concepts in ways the child can see, hear, feel, or touch, if possible. (An example: if a child puts his or her arms around a globe at its widest part the equator can be "felt" and understood better.)

6. *Give children information on anything they want to know, including sex.* Take them to a variety of events so that they know how to behave at each. Practice manners and courtesies. If a child is going to be doing something new, have a "dry run" in advance, maybe a rehearsal at the table for fun.

7. *Make responsibilities and privileges go together.* Have an "Abuse it, you lose it" rule about privileges. Be consistent with discipline and routines, and put the child in responsible positions. As the child grows up, talk ahead of time about the time he or she is expected in; don't wait until just when the child is leaving.

8. *Make positive suggestions, not negative ones.* This can also keep you from saying "no" too often.

9. *Teach older children how to use a pay phone, how to use a road map, how to read ads about events, how to keep a checkbook and savings account.* Have the kind of information that is usually requested on work applications (birth dates, father's occupation, etc.) typed on a card that the young person can carry and refer to. The older child should also know that if stymied by something on a work application, he or she can say, "I'd like to take it home and look it over."

10. *Look for helpful reference materials to keep on hand at home,* such as a low-level easy-reading dictionary and encyclopedia. Easy-reading materials are also available on how to use telephones, read signs, write applications, etc. Many children may need to carry around with them a card on which an alphabet and a calendar are printed.

11. *Don't give up.* Children with learning disabilities may not be ready to learn multiplication tables, decimals, fractions, and percentages in fourth or fifth grade, but they should keep on working at them and know them by ninth or tenth. Cutting up paper plates helps to make fractions easier. Various other math tricks can also help.

12. *Join your school's ACLD chapter, or help to form one if none exists.* Your goals might be:

(1) to help parents exchange experiences and receive information so that they can learn more about their situation, and as a result be more relaxed with, and helpful to, their special children;

(2) to educate others by securing special speakers and films, or by preparing programs that can be taken to church or public service groups in the community;

(3) to work with your school board in securing special education programs for your school;

(4) to help teachers and support them in adapting courses for children with learning disabilities.

The greatest support you can give your child is showing daily that you love and respect him or her for what the child is and for what the child can already do. Your faith in your child is part of your Christian faith.

13

Anne Neufeld Rupp When Your Child
Wants More
Allowance

When our son was in first grade, my husband and I decided
we would begin giving him an allowance. We settled on 50¢ a
week (which was worth somewhat more then than it is now)
with the understanding that this should cover treats,
magazines, and small toys. We also encouraged him to save,
and opened a savings account for him at the local bank.

During the first few weeks he took great pride in keeping
back some money and taking it to the bank teller, who built
up his ego by encouraging him to save. At the same time we as
parents had to close our eyes at the ways in which he "frittered
away" (our evaluation) his allowance. Should we have set
more guidelines? Were there better ways of handling the
allowance question?

A few months later, while we were still asking ourselves
these questions, our son announced, "I need more allowance.
Fifty cents doesn't buy anything!"

What do you do when your child asks for more allowance?

First, parents need to think through the nature of an
allowance, its purpose, and how it is to be set.

Anne Neufeld Rupp, Gossel, Kansas, and her husband Kenneth are copastors of
Alexanderwohl Mennonite Church and the parents of Byron Kenneth.

Money is a medium of exchange. Using money means to learn to make choices. An allowance is intended to give the child some freedom in spending, recognizing that in this way the child can learn to make decision about the use or misuse of money.

Parents can fall into various pitfalls with reference to allowances. Money is powerful, and most of these pitfalls deal with power, because they keep the parents in control. Some of these are:

1. *Parents give an undetermined amount of money only upon request.* This means the child never knows when he or she has had enough, but it empowers a parent to say "no." This keeps control in parental hands.

2. *Parents hinge an allowance on good behavior.* Doyle is an example of a seven-year-old who only receives an allowance if his room has been kept tidy—by whose standards? His allowance becomes something he cannot depend on. It is tied in with behavior or misbehavior. Doyle's allowance becomes a moral issue in which parents use money to express love or disapproval.

3. *Parents give in to requests for money or purchases in addition to the allowance.* When parents "bail out" their children, they are not teaching them responsibility. Granted, there may be occasions for an advance because of a special sale. But the understanding must be that paying off the loan is high priority. If there is an advance, the child will also have to learn to live with the consequences of having less money on hand during the following week.

In any case, a loan or advance is also a parental decision. Parents need to feel okay about saying "no," as well. It is quite in order, when an additional request comes, for the parent to say, "That is to be covered by your allowance."

4. *Parents forget to give the allowance regularly.* A child having to remind his parents not only is put in a dependent, parent-controlled position, but the forgetfulness also indicates to the child that money is not important and can be treated quite irresponsibly.

5. *Parents give the child an allowance but determine exactly how it is to be divided and spent.* This is merely a passing of the parents' money through the child's hands, allowing the child no choice. This is not a child's allowance and again concentrates all control in the parents' hands.

6. *Parents encourage a child to put his or her money into savings for the sake of saving.* This feels safe for the parents, and gives them a sense of control, knowing where the money is. Again this is not the child's money, but the parents.

Now a savings is good for children. But young children must have concrete, attainable goals in saving—a bike, a doll, a toy. They are not capable of saving for college. Psychologists agree that a child who squirrels all his money away, with or without parental encouragement, may have some emotional problems related to security.

Looking at the pitfalls at least helps us determine the nature of an allowance. And whether an allowance should be considered a right or a privilege should be settled at the outset. In any case, it is not wise to use it to sanction one kind of behavior or another. Nor should it be seen as payment for routine work around the house.

But how should allowances be set? When does one begin giving an allowance? What about increases?

One child education consultant states that a child is not ready for an allowance before age 10. Another maintains that eight is a preferable age. Most writers agree that preschool children are not ready for an allowance because they have no sense of the value of money.

So when does one begin? The conclusion I've come to is that it depends on the development of each particular child. Some children can manage money at an earlier age than others. To give a child more or less than he or she is capable of managing at a particular age is unwise. How, then, do you set an allowance that is fair and adequate?

The amount of the allowance should reflect four things: (1) the income and budget of the family, (2) a relation to allowances the child's friends are getting, (3) an assessment of what that allowance is to purchase, and (4) the age as well as the maturity of the child.

If up to the age of nine a child's allowance primarily covers treats and small toys, parents and the child need to decide how much is adequate for this. If parents feel a child is getting responsible enough to carry his or her own lunch money (if they spend it, they miss lunch) or tithe an amount, that should be decided on together, and that amount added to the basic allowance. It is probably wise to test out one additional responsibility at a time as the child matures.

These decisions should not be made arbitrarily by parents but rather in a family council setting. A written budget proposal might be a useful educational tool for the one receiving the allowance as for the rest of the family.

As children get older, they will have more fixed, as well as personal, needs, and the allowance needs to be increased accordingly.

Eventually a child should be ready to handle a comprehensive allowance. This includes everything the family spends on him or her, excluding bed and board. Much of this can already begin at 13, assuming that the young person has been gradually taking on more responsibility between the years 9-12. Parents may want to give monthly allowances so that the young person can budget better. By 15 the young person should have a good idea of how family finances work and through discussion with the family come to a conclusion what a reasonable allowance is.

By the time college comes, young people should be ready to be on their own. One parent says: "When he leaves for college, I will write one check—his total allowance for the year. It will be up to him to bank and budget."

What about a child's own earnings? These should not, it seems to me, affect the allowance. The allowance is the child's or youth's right. If responsibility has been taught all along, the additional earnings will be goal-oriented.

So when a child asks for more allowance, one needs to do more than fork over an extra dime or dollar. One needs to look at the overall picture: income, budget, inflation, the age and sense of responsibility of the child, what that allowance is to buy.

It is almost ten years since we were asked for that increase in allowance. At the time we said, "No." Since then we have said "Yes" numerous times. We have also initiated discussions when we thought it might be time to update the allowance. We never planned a certain percentage increase each year. It became clear to us that needs change not only according to the age, but also the community in which you live. School expenses vary from school to school as well. By now the allowance covers most school, major clothing items, and personal expenses.

Giving allowances is not an easy way out for parents. We've made numerous mistakes over the years. Too often we merely determined the increase in allowance, and used our family council times to discuss our suggestion. Sometimes we forgot to give the allowance, and had to be reminded. At other times, we didn't put enough energy into encouraging goal oriented saving. But we have learned from each situation.

As we give allowances to our children, we must realize that we're not doing it for us. It's much easier for parents if they're in control. We're doing it for the sake of our children. We want to teach them to manage money, not merely use it. Hopefully this will influence not only their spending and saving habits as they mature towards adulthood, but also their commitment to Christian stewardship.

14

Anonymous # When Your Child Wets the Bed

When I was single and would visit in homes where there were young children, I was bothered very much by a peculiar odor. Before I had my family, I firmly decided that the rooms of my children would not have this smell. So one of my preoccupations upon the arrival of my first baby was that he would be dry as much as possible. I changed his diapers as often as necessary and washed everything well.

My child grew up clean. I was proud when soon after he was two years old, he had dry clothes and went to the bathroom by himself.

The years passed, and I didn't even think about wet diapers or other wet clothes. Our second child, a little girl, also learned how to use the bathroom at an early age.

When my son was almost seven years old, I began to notice a faint smell in his bedclothes, especially in his pajamas. But since the bed did not seem stained, I thought it was only a little accident, that he didn't get to the bathroom in time. But the situation became worse. I began to find the bed soaked.

"Cuando su niño moja la cama" ("When your child wets the bed") was written by a woman in Puerto Rico who prefers to remain anonymous so that her son will not be embarrassed. The translation is by Gloria Miller.

I could hardly believe it! How was it possible? At his age! And then I began to suffer the long struggle which has continued for many years: a few "dry" spells interspersed with periods of bed-wetting for no apparent reason.

I have talked to many mothers, some with children older than mine, to get some help. I have also spoken to doctors, pediatricians, psychologists, always trying to find out what I could do. Here are some conclusions I have reached from these years:

1. *You are not the only one who has this problem.* Many parents are experiencing the same thing. Many suffer and worry, but the matter soon passes without major consequences. The majority of mothers and children accept bed-wetting naturally, and it doesn't cause any known difficulties outside of the home. With a few children the problem persists until early adolescence.

2. *Examine your family background.* In my case, I have discovered that my younger sister and brother suffered with bed-wetting until well into adolescence with no lasting consequences. The same happened to my husband's younger brother. Perhaps inheritance has been a subtle influence in my son's problem.

3. *Discard all the advice which well-intentioned people want to give you because it doesn't help.* I tried making the child go without liquids from early evening, but that caused greater restlessness in him because it seems thirst becomes more intense. An alarm by his side did not help either. Everyone else in the household awoke except him. I tried waking him for a time at a certain hour, but the habit became more ingrained because he automatically wet the bed at that hour if I didn't

wake him up. He never completely woke up (even though I got him out of bed) but went to the bathroom like a sleepwalker.

4. *Don't punish the bed wetter.* Many mothers make the child wash the wet clothes. Some parents even mistreat the child, using insulting or scornful language. But anger only creates negative sentiments and complexes in the child.

5. *The best advice which can be given or received is that of acceptance.* Accept the fact, accept the problem—if you consider it a problem. Never try to put diapers on the child as if he were a baby. Help him find confidence in himself. Encourage him. Don't dwell on the subject of bed wetting. If it happens to come up, don't give it much importance.

Find out if there is any emotional problem that may be bothering him. Many times school pressures or small problems at home can cause anxiety in the child that increase the bed-wetting. Help the child to overcome his little conflicts so that he will feel support, tolerance, and understanding. Keep the problem in the home. Don't talk about the matter to outsiders in a way that would embarrass the child, least of all with his friends.

6. *Encourage yourself with the thought that the day will come when the problem will resolve itself.* Then accept it right now: use a mattress pad and keep plenty of extra sheets and pajamas on hand. Teach the child at an early age to make his own bed as part of his daily tasks and teach him to put his sheets and other wet clothes in a designated place. The problem will come to be part of the routine of family living, and eventually it will stop being a problem at all, especially to the life of the child.

15

Roberta Mohr When Your Child Dislikes the Teacher

"My teacher is so mean to me. I hate her!"

What parent hasn't heard that tirade? But what should you do with the statement? Ignore it? Sympathize? March to the principal's office?

Most parents realize they cannot accept as 100 percent true all a child says. Children often exaggerate or honestly misunderstand. So when a child complains about a teacher, the first thing to do is to listen, giving the child the opportunity to talk it out. This may be all the child needs.

Depending on what it is that your child tells you the teacher said or did, you may want to question further: "Is this happening only to you?" "Is it happening every day?" An isolated incident can be overlooked. Everyone has bad days now and then.

One little boy reported to his parents that his teacher was mean, but fair. When asked to explain, he said, "She's mean to everybody." His teacher's "meanness" did not seriously affect him because he had plenty of company. As long as the

---

Roberta Mohr, Wadsworth, Ohio, and her husband Jim are parents of four grown children. After teaching college courses for five years, Roberta has chosen to return to her first love—small children—and now teaches kindergarten in the Wadsworth City Schools. A pastor's wife (First Mennonite, Wadsworth), Roberta is on the Board of Education and Publication of the Central District of her denomination.

90

students in that class could support each other, they could struggle through a threatening situation. But when a child feels alone, as though he or she is being singled out for the teacher's harsh treatment, there is a definite problem.

Sometimes children have difficulty talking about their anxiety, but they signal for help in other ways. If your child vomits each morning before the school bus arrives or invents a different reason each day for staying home from school, investigate further. While an occasional feigned illness is not unusual (particularly if there is a big test that day), a daily plea to stay home merits further examination.

An even more serious sign is an emotional one, such as a change in personality. A normally happy, outgoing child may become quiet and withdrawn or a pleasant child irritable and even hostile.

It is extremely important not to jump to conclusions and make comments to your child about the teacher. Refrain from criticizing the teacher or speaking disparagingly in any way.

When you have decided that your child definitely has cause for disliking a teacher, your first step is to arrange a meeting with the teacher personally. Discussing it with others first is unwise. The "grapevine" operates well, and the teacher may hear something that will cause defensiveness when you finally approach him or her. You and the school should resolve these matters in private.

If a conference is necessary, be fair. Avoid hasty conclusions and damaging statements. Affairs at school as told to you by your child may seem to be a certain way as you view it from your home, but the real situation may be far different when you see it factually in the school setting.

You may also decide to visit the class in action. Younger children are delighted to have their mothers or fathers in the classroom; older children would rather die. Be sensitive to your child's feelings about a visit before you make plans for one.

Suppose during your conference or your visit to the classroom you discover that your child is right. The teacher really *is* mean. No one ever promised that your child would be taught by a model teacher. There are a number of bad teachers in schools—for a variety of reasons.

One elderly teacher told me she can hardly wait for retirement. When she chose a career, it was either to be a nurse or a teacher. Since she couldn't stand the sight of blood, she chose teaching, though she has never particularly enjoyed it; but "it's a job."

Some younger teachers blame their rotten disposition on the children. "You have to get mean before they pay attention. If I smiled, they'd run all over me," one teacher said. Fortunately, there are many smiling teachers who still run an orderly classroom and have both the love and respect of their pupils. I even know one who actually prays for each student individually before she leaves her classroom each afternoon.

On the other hand, you may find your child's teacher is not really "mean," just different. The teacher's personality may not be one that your child finds compatible.

Some educators believe that a child is stronger for being in a class with such a teacher. This is especially true in older grades, where children are preparing for junior high school. Teenagers find that a variety of teachers, many of whom they dislike, is a cold fact of life, and they must simply stick it out and learn to cope. But in the primary grades, much depends on the personality of the child. Not all children grow stronger from a bad experience; for some it is devastating.

My neighbor's daughter, Lisa, a first-grader, complained of stomach aches each morning and insisted she was too sick to go to school. Whenever her parents allowed her to stay home, however, she remained tearful and upset all day. She worried that her teacher would be angry with her for missing school and that she would have to make up the work during recess.

As the weeks went by, Lisa would burst into tears at even the slightest reprimand by her parents. She became quieter and more withdrawn at home. Her actions made friends and relatives ask what was wrong.

One month into the school year should be enough to make a judgment. Lisa's parents waited until the end of the first nine-week marking period. They arranged for a conference with the teacher, who expressed genuine surprise that there was any trouble. Lisa was a "good little girl" who did what she was told. Her classwork was average. As far as the teacher was concerned, no problem existed; it was entirely the little girl's (or her parents') fantasy.

Lisa's parents, who were both educators themselves, hesitated to push, knowing how teachers feel about parents who interfere too much in the lives of their children. Nevertheless, they felt something was definitely out of the ordinary.

Gradually, through talking with Lisa and visiting the classroom, they pieced things together. When the teacher reprimanded the children who didn't have their work finished, Lisa wasn't sure whether her work was finished or not and assumed she was being scolded. Because children who talked out of turn were punished, Lisa was afraid she might inadvertently say something at the wrong time and consequently began to say less and less, even at home. She became more and more withdrawn in order to avoid doing all the things that evoked a frown or rebuke from the teacher.

Lisa's mother noticed that others in the class seemed more self-confident. They either knew they had done nothing wrong and the teacher was not yelling at them, or they realized they deserved the teacher's discipline.

At the end of the second nine-week marking period, Lisa's parents again expressed a concern to the teacher and told her they were taking the matter to the principal. In retrospect they wish they had not waited so long.

They told the principal only of Lisa's resistance to going to school each morning and her behavior at home. They refrained from placing any blame on the teacher or even hinting that they thought she was at fault.

The principal suggested a psychological test, which revealed their daughter was developmentally immature. Because Lisa's present teacher was a strict disciplinarian with a sober, nononsense approach to teaching, the principal decided to put Lisa in another first-grade classroom. He chose a more gentle, understanding teacher with a warm personality. This second teacher remarked to the parents that Lisa seemed "scared to death" the first week.

Gradually Lisa regained her self-confidence and began to enjoy going to school. Together the parents and teacher decided Lisa should remain in first grade another year to "catch up" developmentally.

If the principal had been uncooperative, what would have been the next step? There are other professionals, such as the guidance counsellor and the school psychologist, to whom you could go for advice. They can visit the classroom and observe the interaction between your child and the teacher. They are trained to talk with children in a nonthreatening manner in order to obtain desired information. They can then make a recommendation to the principal, which carries the weight of their professional experience.

Educators disagree on whether children can bounce back after a year in a stressful situation. I tend to believe they can if they have a good self-concept and good support from home.

I asked my son, who had a rough third-grade experience, if

he remembered his third-grade teacher. He said, "Sure. She was fat and ugly."

Further questioning revealed, however, that he didn't remember much else about that year. When I poked his memory, stirring up recollections of incidents that caused us both many sleepless nights, he commented, "Well, it must not have affected me very much, because I don't remember any of it."

I believe it was the support we provided at home in maintaining his self-concept that helped him forget a teacher who was so critical of his every action that she made even an "A" seem like punishment.

As a parent, you know your child's personality better than anyone else. If you suspect your child is in a situation that is potentially damaging, seek help quickly by talking first to the teacher. But if you see the situation as an opportunity for your child to grow in his understanding of others and his ability to adapt to new situations, challenge your child with this possibility while you continue to build up a good self-concept at home. Parents can make all the difference in whether a specific teacher makes or breaks your child.

16

Phyllis R. and Rex V. Naylor When Your Child
Stutters

Most parents want their children to be proficient in whatever is important to their self-respect, be it swimming or singing or speaking. Many, at some time during a child's development, are concerned about speech: he talks too fast; she talks too loud; he hesitates, stops, or starts over. For children learning to talk, this is normal and will gradually decrease as they get more practice in speaking.

But some children create a strange struggle with words, and parents want desperately to help. Common sense tells them that one who stutters needs to learn to talk smoothly and fluently, that the parents' job is to help stop repetitions and hesitations. In this case, common sense couldn't be more wrong.

At least part of the time, a person who stutters can say easily the words which at other times prove difficult. A child might sing in the bathtub and do fine. A child can stand in an empty church and read five chapters of Genesis without a blocking once. But let someone walk in, and the trouble begins. Stuttering is not only a speech problem; it is also a problem of social interaction.

Phyllis and Rex Naylor live in Bethesda, Maryland, and are the parents of two grown sons. Phyllis, a free-lance writer, is author of more than 50 books. Dr. Naylor, who holds a Ph.D. in speech pathology, recently retired as Chief of Speech Pathology at the Naval Medical Center in Bethesda.

Hence the person who stutters does not need to learn to say words smoothly. He or she already knows how to do that. The goal is to learn to talk disfluently in a normal fashion.

Stuttering is a way of holding back while going ahead—talking with the brakes on. In an effort to keep from tripping over a word, stuttering children hold their breath, tense their muscles, or "freeze" their mouths in one position. Instead of stumbling through a word calmly and effortlessly as most of us do, they make a big production of it. Because they feel embarrassed or afraid of what people will think, they may hold in the word until they feel they can say it perfectly. They may substitute another word for the one they fear. But they defeat their own purpose. In the long run they are more disfluent than ever—conspicuously so, because they make such a struggle of it.

The problem, then, is to retrain the person who stutters to handle disfluent speech the way other people handle it—in a calm, relaxed manner. The child should not try to eliminate disfluencing—just make it better, and easier.

When a child's speech becomes a real problem, other problems may develop as well. Stuttering children not only feel bad about the way they talk, they may feel disgusted with themselves as persons. They may see themselves as stutterers, not simply as persons who sometimes stutter; all other good qualities are overshadowed—for them—by their halting speech. The more they feel disliked because of it, the more tense and perfectionistic they become.

What can parents do to help? If your child is just beginning to stutter or shows little awareness of the problem, it is vitally important to do nothing to call attention to it. If the child is quite young, you may be mistaking normal disfluency for stuttering. But if it is stuttering, a speech pathologist may prefer working indirectly with the problem through you.

An older child will probably get help from the school speech pathologist. If your school does not have one, you may obtain names from your local hospital or university speech clinic, or the American Speech-Language-Hearing Association, 10801 Rockville Pike, Rockville, Md. 20852.

When an older child begins treatment, he or she may be given opportunities to practice stuttering easily. "Stutter more, not less," may be the rule, and don't be surprised if stuttering seems to worsen temporarily as the child grapples with it instead of trying to hide it. The trained professional will help the child work through muscle tension as well as negative emotional feelings.

You should never praise a child for speaking without stuttering. That only makes the child more anxious about the times stuttering does occur. Nor should a child be punished, ridiculed, pitied, or given suggestions about talking or breathing. Instead, praise the child for stuttering easily and casually, and pay no attention to how frequently it happens. Build the feeling that your child is a worthwhile person who can afford to stutter a bit. Other people hesitate and repeat and mispronounce and get by with it; so can your child.

Most important of all is an atmosphere of love and acceptance in the home. The child should be shown often that he or she is loved, and parents should keep the home as free from tension, criticism, and undue excitement as possible. Simply slowing down the tempo of the household may help. At the same time, the stuttering children need opportunities to express themselves, particularly angry feelings, and to build self-confidence and a sense of achievement.

If a child is ever going to conquer fear of stuttering, that child must do it while stuttering. Though the child should perhaps never be forced to speak, he or she should be strongly encouraged. If Billy's Sunday school class has never asked him to read the Scripture because he stutters, maybe now is the time to begin. Billy needs to learn that the roof won't fall in if he repeats a few times.

Even if he botches the job completely, Billy needs to realize that he is still the best artist in the class or a good swimmer or simply a nice guy to have around. And the next time he tells you that he doesn't want to talk with company or say grace at the table because he stutters, your reaction can be a simple, "So what if you do?" The person who stutters is likely to be frightened and embarrassed by disfluency, so much that the child may even feel stuttering is uncontrollable. But, of course, it isn't.

If Billy has never discussed his problem with the rest of the family, you might help him get it out in the open. Encourage him to tell the others his feelings about stuttering and seek their reaction. He may find, surprisingly, that others aren't half as concerned about it as he is.

While parents should not protect their child from average situations in which the child is required to talk, it is their duty to protect the child when possible from ridicule. A talk with the child's teachers can help, so that you and they can plan how to handle Billy's problem consistently, and how to explain it to other children when necessary.

It is too much to expect, however, that the son or daughter who stutters will never be teased or laughed at. In fact, humor may be an ally, and the stuttering child who is relaxed enough to laugh at his or her own fumblings may well be on the way to speaking more easily and openly. One thing Billy needs to learn is that he gives his listeners clues as to how they should react. If he stands on one foot and then another, blinks his eyes, clenches his fists, mops his brow, and stares at the floor while he stutters, he simply suggests to his friends that they, too, should be embarrassed or should feel sorry for him.

Chances are they will fidget uneasily and look away. If Billy smiles easily and tolerantly at his own blocking, his audience may also learn to treat it casually.

If your child's problem is typical, there are a hundred ways to avoid stuttering, and you probably make matters worse without knowing it. You may find yourself finishing a sentence to help your child get it over with. Maybe you supply the word Billy's struggling so hard to pronounce or drop your eyes when he stutters. Perhaps he even cons you into making his phone calls for him. But he must learn to face trouble himself.

When Billy's feeling worst about himself, don't keep reassuring him that he will be able to talk better one of these days. Take him as he is. Help him realize that he is not a freak, that there is no way in which his stuttering need hurt either him or your love for him.

Stuttering is not a disease, and it is not inherited. Though males who stutter vastly outnumber females, the problem has affected both sexes and all classes of society, including such prominent persons as Sir Winston Churchill. And the person who stutters is definitely not alone. There are around two million others just in the United States. It is foolish to keep the problem hidden, since this is the kind of behavior that thrives on concealment. Successful treatment requires not only a step toward freer speech; it requires a step toward maturity. And loving parents can help their child take that step.

17

Jane P. Moyer When Your Child
Hates Her Name

"Hello, Moyers'? Is Diane there?"

"Diane?" Surely someone must have the wrong number.

"Diane Moyer," the child's voice answered.

"Oh! You mean Robin. Hold on. I'll call her."

That was the end of that conversation. But later when school messages came home to the parents of Diane Moyer, I checked with our daughter about the name change. I found that she had told her teachers and classmates that her name was Diane. Since it was her first year in this school, it had been easy for her to change to her middle name.

Retraining her father and me was much harder. For one thing, we both felt a bit miffed that she hated her first name. Choosing her name hadn't been a spur of the moment decision. We had been so pleased when we came up with Robin Diane. We thought it had just the right sound.

Now it became quite annoying to us to find that every time we used Robin our requests were ignored. Or we were told straightforwardly that the name is Diane, thank you.

The reasons for the change were quite clear. Someone at

Jane P. Moyer, her husband Dave, and their daughter Diane live at Lancaster, Pennsylvania. They attend First Deaf Mennonite Church. Jane is the administrator of New Danville Mennonite School (kindergarten through grade 8).

school had teased her about Robin Redbreast just once too often. Besides, who wanted a name that could even be a boy's! To a second-grader, the logic was incontestable.

I found it easier to be tolerant when I thought of my own name. Even though my parents named me after a favorite aunt, I could never stand the name, and I changed to my middle name sometime in junior high. At that time, I thought there would be no way to misspell and mispronounce Jane. Unfortunately, I forgot about all the things that rhyme with it.

Curious as to how many kids are encumbered with names they don't appreciate, I asked 57 of my high school students if they disliked their names. Twenty answered "yes." Their reasons varied. Several mentioned that their names were too original. They would have liked more common, popular names. Another disliked his because it was so easy to make nicknames with. One boy hated his because it was the same as his father's. Last names were a problem, too. One thought his was too long, and another didn't like the meaning of his.

Psychologists and educators have found that names can help or hinder the development of a good self-image and friendships and may even affect success in school or on the job. People tend to associate certain characteristics with a particular name. When a British psychologist asked persons to rank names according to attractiveness, trustworthiness, and sociability, he found that Johns are seen to be trustworthy and kind; Robins are young; Tonys, sociable; Agneses, old; Agneses and Matildas, unattractive; and Anns, nonaggressive. Psychologist E. D. Lawson's study of common names yielded similar results. College students saw common names as better, stronger, and more active than unusual ones.

Teachers may be influenced in their evaluations by the name of the child. Researchers Harari and McDavid had teachers grade essays written by fifth-graders. They chose desirable and undesirable names to identify the essays. Essays written by students with names such as Elmer, Bertha, and Hubert consistently received the lowest grades.

But lest all the Zacharys and Gwendolyns despair, in 1977 psychologist Zweigenhaft questioned the validity of earlier research. Feeling there may have been additional data not yet considered, he set out to find out how social class, sex, and race influenced a name's effects. He found that among the upper classes having an unusual name was no hindrance. Among upper-class white males an unusual name might even be an asset. But for the economically underprivileged black female the unusual name might work just the opposite effect.

Studies done at Temple and Tulane universities yielded a list of desirable and undesirable names. Desirable names for boys include Craig, David, Gregory, James, Jeffery, Jonathan, John, Michael, Patrick, Richard, Robert, Steven, and Thomas. Desirable girls' names include Barbara, Carol, Cindy, Diane, Dorothy, Jane, Karen, Linda, Lisa, and Virginia. Undesirable names for boys, according to these studies, are Albert, Bernard, Chester, Curtis, Darrell, Elmer, Gerald, Henry, Horace, Hubert, Jerome, Maurice, Roderick, and Samuel. Undesirable names for girls are Bertha, Bergit, Gillian, Hallie, Hillary, Lola Mae, Mildred, Phoebe, Risa, and Simone.

Concern over the appropriateness of children's names is not a recent development. As far back as 1760, Burn's Ecclesiastical Law in England stated that "the ministers shall take care not to permit wanton names, which being pronounced, do sound to (sic) lasciviousness, to be given to children baptized, especially of the female sex: and if otherwise done, the name shall be changed by the bishop at confirmation."

Probably the record for parental indecision in choosing a name for an offspring is held by the parents of a girl born in

Liverpool in December 1880. They named her Anna Bertha Cecilia Diana Emily Fanny Gertrude Hypatia Inez Jane Kate Louise Maud Nora Ophelia (The "P" is found in the last name.) Quence Rebecca Starkey Teresa Ulysis Venus Winifred Xenophon Yetty Zeno Pepper. At least they deserve credit for alphabetizing it for easy reference.

What do parents do when they find they have made a mistake and their child really hates his or her name? There are several alternatives. If the child has a middle name that he or she likes, the simplest thing is to use that and drop the offensive first name. I can attest that this works well.

There are some difficulties. For one thing, it means a lifetime of bucking forms that demand a first name and middle initial. Also, the law recognizes only one Christian name. A middle name or initial are not considered indisputable means of identifying a person. If the middle name isn't used consistently there are other problems, too. I've ended up defending my honesty while a skeptical clerk waited for an explanation of a driver's license that gave one combination and a check that listed another.

If neither name is desirable, a nickname might provide an answer. I've known Butches who were really Dons, Chucks who were Rons, as well as persons who merely shortened unwieldy names like Christopher to Chris.

Of course, some persons have just the opposite problem. They love their real names, but in adolescent years are still tagged with baby endearments such as Punkin', Toots, and Missy. Diminutives such as Timmy, Paulie, and Billy are soon outgrown.

A much more complete solution to the name problem is to legally change one's name. Actually, it's a rather simple procedure. Edward Bander in his book *Change of Name and Law of Names* gives a thorough explanation. Under common law a person may change his name as often as he wants, as long as it is not for an illegal or fraudulent purpose, without seeking a court's permission (with the exception of the states of Pennsylvania and Oklahoma). There may be some legal complications arising from this method, and many people prefer to follow the statutory procedure because they want to have a record of their name change.

In that case, they make an application to a court of law or public officer stating the new name and reasons for the change. In some states a hearing is held and a petition must be published in the newspaper. In most states the parents must sign if the person is under 21 years of age. In some states a copy of the court order is given to the bureau of vital statistics in the state and a correction is made of the birth certificate.

If none of these solutions sounds viable, the situation is not hopeless. Children and adults need to be reminded that when Solomon said that a good name is more to be desired than great riches, he was likely referring to a spotless reputation. Many persons have made valuable contributions despite an unattractive and unpopular name.

18

N. Gerald Shenk When Your Child
Is Afraid
of Communists

Alert beyond his young years, our friend Joel was troubled with a question he needed to check out with his parents. On the way home from the farewell service for my wife and me, headed for several years of study and work in Yugoslavia, Joel asked, "But aren't there communists there?"

While hovering about the small-town barbershop which his father operated, Joel likely had overheard conversations among the customers. From them he learned that blame for all things threatening to our lifestyle and future on this planet is to be laid at the feet of conspiratorial communists.

From his own church library Joel may have read religious fiction in which revolutions make refugees. These were commemorated as another chapter in the lengthy tradition of harried departures in search of religious freedom.

But if Joel's consciousness of communism was being formed by the culture around him, the most powerful association with the idea *communist* probably comes from the threat of nuclear holocaust. At Joel's age, my own fears were focused by the Cuban missile confrontation and the Bay of Pigs. As

N. Gerald Shenk, and his wife Sara, parents of Joseph and Timothy, continue their multiethnic involvements in Evanston, Illinois, with Reba Place Church. Gerald is a Ph.D. candidate in religious studies at Northwestern University, with a focus on religious communities in socialist societies.

best I could tell then, the world was about to be blown away, because *they* were misbehaving.

What is a child to do with the weight of these horrors on his shoulders? Too young then to evaluate facts for myself, I was nevertheless gripped by the lurid alarms which insistently urged the populace to make the world free by winning the arms race.

The statistics came and went. Every month another retired general was commissioned to cobble up a fresh set of figures and prove that the strategic situation was much worse than last month. You know how to read those dramatic little diagrams at a glance. But do you remember how they affect the young readers digestion?

My preteen imagination had me pausing from my work in secret panic to strain for glimpses of red stars on the jet fighters every time they terrorized the Pennsylvania skies in formation during war games over the potato fields. *Their* planes or *ours?* No matter to whom they belonged, it was enough to make a kid shiver on the hottest day in August!

Even today the child in me tunes in those notes of insecurity. I still want to shriek when those jets play death overhead. But I have learned that insecurity is what builds and fuels them, on both sides of conflict. And once the bombs and bullets are actually used, it's too late to discover their ideological commitments.

The magazines and news programs available in our homes have a different impact on children than they do on adults. Young readers are not naturally equipped with those adult filters which help detect manipulation and resist propaganda. The youngster's heart strings are plucked readily enough when "life as we know it" and "the very survival of the American way of life" seem to be at stake. But he or she does not know that those authoritative articles are written by experts who depend (just like their budgets) on the climate of fear and hostility they engender. Their primary target is not children. They write for taxpayers and voters, since these must bear the burden of new and more expensive weapons systems.

But one can do more for children than just to fit them with adult filters to screen out propaganda with a healthy measure of skepticism. By far my own most effective resources against fear and insecurity were provided by my family and faith community, where a really different picture of the world was being subtly cultivated along with the potatoes. There some vital perspectives were bent hard against the prevailing winds of popular opinion. I believe now this is counterculture at its best.

Within such a framework, there's much that can be done to help children face apparent threats from communists, from others. Here are some ideas I believe they can grasp as these are taught to them:

1. *Peoplehood is too precious to be split on national or racial lines.* The foundational reality here is fellowship in Christ, the one people of God. Are the Russians coming? This unspoken terror lost most of its sway for me that memorable day when they really came, right into the heart of our quiet community. A delegation of Russian Christians spoke in our churches under the auspices of the Mennonite Central Committee. That dramatic demonstration of Christian fellowship across the political and national chasms etched itself on my young mind.

Already then the we-they split began to shift. I had to draw it a different way, even before I ever heard of nationalism.

2. *Security is too crucial to be entrusted to the merchants of fear and weapons.* Neither the home nor the faith community can ultimately be protected by relying on might. The interests

which drive the engines of war and geopolitics are economic, imperial, and demonic in any sober biblical analysis. When the Caesars frost up a new cold war, stir up bitter nationalist hatred, and launch their destructive might from one side of the planet to the other, we derive no comfort and no security whatsoever from this.

"Security" and war-minded people will most certainly continue to build their planes, missiles, and bombs on both sides. All such efforts are the same for us: useless. Our purposes in the international fellowship of the body of the risen Lord must be different, must be directed to life, must give testimony to the peace which was made for us already on the cross. Here a defense industry has no business at all.

3. *Communism is too good to be left to the atheists.* The ideals of a just social order, cooperative work, and a fair distribution of essential goods and services were not invented in the reading room of the British Museum in nineteenth-century London by a bushy-bearded German exile named Karl Marx. But history must credit him with prophetically resurrecting those ideals from the Judeo-Christian tradition and greatly disturbing the whole of decadent Christendom with them.

What's more, were the communitarian values of our own tradition written large enough to pertain to a whole society, they would have much in common with these same goals. Though we differ from the Marxists on how to overcome the real and systemic injustices of our world, we must not abandon the field to them. Retiring to sanctuaries of inner piety would betray our own biblical mandates for peace and justice.

4. *Communist countries are too varied to blame them all for the superpower conflict.* This is admittedly of lesser import, but the

brush with catastrophe at the Three Mile Island nuclear facility made it clear to me that those potato fields of my childhood in Pennsylvania are far more vulnerable to our local power company than to attack from Yugoslavia, for example. This country, in fact, has a heritage of more than 1,200 years of straddling the ancient tensions between East and West. Today its foreign policy is directed to the politics of nonalignment.

This means that with more than one hundred other nations Yugoslavia seeks reduced tensions, disarmament, and a more just economic order in international relations. Little boys in Pennsylvania need not fear this. But it would be helpful if their parents could introduce them to these truly international concerns and efforts.

There are then some practical guidelines for relating with your children to this source of anxiety.

Be in touch with the development of your child's thinking about the world. Be able to speak openly and realistically about the problems which face humankind. To belittle or deny them isn't helpful. Be wary of the simplistic formulas which substitute for serious explanation of international conflicts. Neither the blame nor the solutions can be one-sided.

Be jealous of the sources of information which come regularly into your home. Subscribe to at least one magazine which provides alternative awareness of world events. How does a certain development affect little nations, the poor, the starving? What are Christians in other parts of the world trying to tell North Americans?

Followers of Jesus are urged to pray for all—for kings and all who are in high places (1 Tim. 2). Yet when the Caesars lead their people into conflict with each other, as is their habit, those crusades do not belong to the Jesus way. Especially then you must be teaching your children to pray soberly about those who endanger so many. Pray together about the fear this strikes into both big and little people. Do not forget that these events are the consequences of actual people who make real decisions.

Build personal and congregational ties with believers who have chosen to live out their Christian commitments in a socialist context. If you make pilgrimages to the memory spots of faith history in Western Europe, do not hesitate to visit the socialist part of the continent as well. Faith history continues to be written here, in conditions no less complex than those of the irretrievable sixteenth-century Reformation. Short tours cannot remold the perspectives formed by years of mass media, but you can convince yourself that a normal life is available, and that believers face the same range of essential decisions as you do.

Yes, Joel, I can assure you there are communists in Yugoslavia. I'm glad you know that much about the world you live in. But be sure to know that Christians live here too, and they outnumber any other group in the country. Their task, like yours when you grow up, is to make a positive contribution to overcoming the hate and mistrust which separate people from each other—and ultimately from God.

19

Kenneth L. Gibble ## When Your Child Has Doubts

"Who never doubted,
never half believed."
—Philip James Bailey

How does it start?

Maybe your seventh-grader seems exceptionally quiet at the supper table one evening. When you ask if there's anything wrong, he mutters, "Nah. I'm okay." But you can tell *something* is bothering him.

Later on that evening, maybe while you're doing the dishes, he comes out with it. "Mom, how did God create the world?"

Your first inclination is to say, "Why, just as it says in the book of Genesis." But you suspect he wants more than a quick answer. Instead you say, "What makes you ask, son?"

"Well, our science teacher says that it took millions and millions of years for the earth just to be made and then millions of more years for life to happen and even millions more till man arrived. And he says that we weren't really created; we 'evolved.' And, Mom, if that's true—" here he

---

Kenneth L. Gibble and his wife Ann copastor the Arlington, Virginia, Church of the Brethren, and are parents of Katie. Kenneth's articles have appeared in more than 70 different magazines. He is author of five books and of several plays.

stops to look at you with solemn eyes—"then what about what the Bible says?"

When this happens, you know this situation is different from the kind of questions your child asked when he was smaller. If as a youngster he asked, "What does God look like?" or "Why was Jesus killed?" you knew that, difficult as those questions were, you could answer them with some confidence. Back then, your child asked such questions out of natural curiosity. And he accepted you as *the* authority on such matters because you were the all-wise, all-knowing adult figure in his life.

But now the situation is different. Your child has begun to realize that some adults know more about certain subjects than you do. And that troubles him. Who *is* the authority? he has begun to wonder. It's become an insecure world in which adults don't agree on all the answers. So your son's question to you is motivated not by the innocent curiosity of childhood but by something entirely new—and frightening to both you and him. His question has been prompted by doubt.

The first time doubt appears, it's only natural for us who are parents to feel upset, disappointed, or threatened. We may be angry at the teacher who has raised questions in our child's mind or at the author of a book which has done the same thing. We may consider the possibility of censoring our child's reading from now on or confronting that teacher at school to demand a stop to the destroying of our child's faith.

But when we calm down a bit, we know that such extreme measures would be neither practical nor wise. Though knowing our child no longer will take everything we say as gospel truth is a bit of a blow to our self-esteem, we've known all along that one day it would come to this. And, in one sense, we welcome it, realizing our child has progressed one more step on the long road to maturity.

All the same, we parents wonder how to handle the expressions of doubt from our children. Should we defend the Bible and Christian doctrine? Should we just ignore the questions by saying, "Don't worry about such things; when you're older, you'll understand it better"? What is the right way to deal with children's doubts?

A starting point could be a quiet time in which we as parents think back to our own experiences with doubt. Can we recall the first time we questioned our own parents' judgment on an issue? How did we feel? How did they react? Are there lessons we can learn from those experiences?

As I reflected on some of my doubts during my student days, I realized that what I most wanted from my folks at that point was their understanding of what I was going through. I didn't expect them to change their beliefs to accommodate my changing views of things. In fact, I would have been disappointed if they had changed. There was a certain security in knowing that their faith wasn't going to cave in just because I was troubled by doubts about God and the Bible and Christian beliefs.

On the other hand, I didn't want them to discount or deny the disturbing thoughts that were running through my head. It didn't help me to be told that I shouldn't even *ask* certain questions, that some things had to be accepted on faith.

Probably the best thing we parents can do for our children when they express doubts is to listen willingly. It's a compliment when children talk to us about their questions, and we ought to express appreciation for the trust they've expressed in us. Then, if it seems appropriate, we can affirm their trust by telling them that we remember coming to our own parents with similar questions. This affirmation will allow our children to feel that expressing their doubts to us is acceptable, that they aren't committing a sin by having questions in their minds, that every Christian has doubts from time to time.

How should we listen? By learning to stop talking, first of all. Our tendency as parents is to offer quick, reassuring answers to our child's questions about faith. So when daughter Lisa asks, "If all those miracles described in the Bible really did happen, how come such miracles never happen now?" we want to jump in to allay her fears with the best possible answer. Part of our anxiety may stem from the fact that she has put into words a doubt which we have never resolved ourselves!

Instead of giving a quick answer to Lisa, we can be more helpful to her by gently probing a bit deeper. This could take the form of questions or comments: "Are there other things about the Bible that are bothering you?" or "I can tell you've been giving some really serious thought to this."

Such responses on our part are an invitation to Lisa to go a step further. Maybe the question about miracles is really all she's struggling with. On the other hand, it may be only one expression of doubt about the church or about whom to trust or about any number of things. By learning to listen, we can help our children give voice to their deepest feelings.

Most of us, however, will not feel comfortable with merely listening. There does come a time, I believe, when parents should express their convictions. But there are at least two ways of doing it:

1. *"Now look, Lisa, you've been reared in a fine Christian home* and we've always been a church family. You're just going to have to learn to accept that what the Bible says is true."

2. *"Well, Lisa, I've gone through times of questioning and doubting too.* We all do. But here's where I come out on this issue. I believe that. . . . "

This second way of expressing our beliefs can accomplish several things. It assures Lisa that her doubts have not destroyed our faith, even though hers may be badly shaken. It tells her that she's still okay, even though she is questioning her faith. And it allows her freedom to find her own answers rather than demanding that she subscribe to ours.

Many parents, when confronted with their child's doubts, will turn to someone else for counsel—sometimes a church friend, sometimes the minister. This allows others to provide the ministry of Christian support and concern. It can be helpful to hear how other parents have dealt with the problem— and how they weathered the storm.

However, each child is different. What "worked" with our friends' children may not be helpful in our situation. Rather than adopt someone else's way of handling things, it is better to relate to our child as a person in his or her own right.

There may come a point at which we'll want to suggest that our child talk to someone—again perhaps our minister or someone whose Christian maturity both we and our child respect. This step should not be taken as a last, desperate measure: "I give up! Go talk to the pastor!" Rather, it should be an opportunity for our child to confide in someone with whom he or she can talk freely. The inescapable truth is that, as open as parents are to hearing their child's questions, most children hesitate to be completely candid with Mom and Dad because to express doubt may make them appear to be ungrateful offspring. It can be an immense relief for a child to find a person outside the family whose own faith is strong, someone who can listen to his or her doubts without feeling threatened.

Finally, we must remember that doubts are often the stepping-stones to a mature faith. In order for our children to grow spiritually, they need to study, question, and reflect on the meaning of life and faith. We can help point the way to growth by suggesting helpful books, by having them subscribe to a good Christian youth magazine, by encouraging them to attend Bible studies and youth classes at church. Family discussion sessions about biblical teachings and Christian values can become a weekly activity in our homes.

None of these suggestions will eliminate doubts in our children. But they can be positive influences for helping them find their answers during times of questioning.

20

Hope Lind — When Your Child Starts the First Job

Our 15-year-old son, Myron, hung up the phone. "They're extra busy at Collins and wonder if I'd like to work until school starts."

He was casual about it, matter-of-fact. I was excited. Collins is probably the most respected bicycle sales and repair shop in our area. It had been Myron's dream to get a job there when he was old enough. Now they were asking him to help.

"Why didn't you tell them you could start right away, like this afternoon?" I thought Myron should hurry right in, show them he was eager to work. After all, it's not easy for teenagers to find jobs. That year the unemployment rate for teenagers was 12.2 percent, compared to the adult rate of 6.4 percent.

Instead, Myron went in to talk about the job, telling them he could start tomorrow. He continued working there most summers until he graduated from college.

When your child lands a job, then what? How can you be confident that he understands all that is involved in the job and does good work? What will be his transportation? What kind of adjustments must you make in your family schedule

Hope Lind, Eugene, Oregon, and her husband Cliff are the parents of Janet, Myron, Julia, and Carl. Hope frequently reviews books and is writing a history of Oregon Mennonites.

and work details at home? How will decisions be made about the way his earnings are spent?

At least two things provide a good background for getting a job and then doing it well. One is learning to be responsible in work around home. Another is developing skills in a variety of areas.

If your child has learned to share in the work of the household—preparing food, cleaning, doing laundry, maintaining the yard, and other mundane affairs—he will likely be able to move into the responsibilities his new employment entails. Children who are part of a family in which work is viewed as honorable, essential, and even enjoyable (at least *some* of the time) will likely have positive attitudes about their jobs. And if a job does turn out to be dull, boring, a drag, it won't last forever. The next job will probably be better.

If you provide a wide range of work and recreational experiences for your child, he will have a better chance of getting a job and finding success in it. My husband, Cliff, who has made himself handy at just about anything, took our children on long bike rides even when they were very young. (Sometimes he overestimated their endurance and had to tow them up the last long hill with a rope.) He has done most of the maintenance and repairs on his own bicycle and he taught Myron the elementary aspects of it. When the job opportunity came along for Myron, he was able to move right in and become a valued worker.

All of our four children helped on the construction of our new church building. When Janet, as a high school graduate, learned of a possible job helping someone build fences and decks, she knew enough about construction to get the short-term summer job.

Depending upon where you live, transportation to work can be a problem. If your child does not have a driver's

license, you may decide to take him to the job and pick him up
again. That can get old quickly. However, a girl (or a boy)
who works in a restaurant or at another job until late at night
may need to have a parent pick her (him) up.

Even if your teenager is a driver, you may not be able or
choose to schedule the car for his routine driving to work.
Perhaps car-pooling or using the city bus is a possibility. Or
what about such self-locomotion as walking or bicycling, at
least some of the time? Since Cliff regularly uses his bicycle for
transportation to work, our children did not usually feel taken
advantage of when they also had to bike to their jobs.

When your child gets a job, it is one more thing to fit into
what is probably already a full schedule. He is likely to
continue some or all of his recreational interests even while
holding the job. This may mean there are days when the
family does not eat even one meal together. But nothing goes
on forever. Play practice will end in a few weeks, the soccer
season will be over after a while, the job schedule may change.
Or you may have to rearrange your expectations and establish
a new normalcy.

We found it difficult to fit our children's home responsibilities into the schedule when they were on the job all day.
The simple fact is that when Myron arrived home just in time
to sit down at the supper table, there was no way he could help
prepare the meal. Still, if he ate with the family, he *could* help
do the dishes now and then. And sometimes in his schedule, if
we insisted, he did find a time to clean his own room, at least
once in a while.

It's our position, Cliff's and mine, that being part of a
family does entail responsibilities for everyone. We are
concerned that home be more than a place to eat what someone else *always* prepares, sleep in sheets that someone else *always* changes, and lounge in a house that someone else *always*

cleans. While we did try to switch details in the family division of labor, how the labor was divided became less important to us, especially during job season, than making sure it was divided.

Deciding how earnings are to be used may be easy or difficult. It could be helpful for parents and child to have a general understanding about earnings even before the first paycheck is issued. Should the child now be responsible for buying his own clothes? How much should he be encouraged to give to the church? What percentage or amount should be put into savings for college or such future needs? How much can he be justified in spending for his hobbies? Should you, the parents, have the veto power on major money decisions? To attempt answers to such questions, Cliff helped Myron build a simple budget, balancing his projected earnings with his savings and major spendings.

Ideally, children should be able to exercise considerable freedom and responsibility in these matters. Realistically, parents may decide that a particular child needs help in money management for a time.

Regardless of how much or little parental involvement there is, the child should be held accountable for his decisions, both for his personal development and future fiscal solvency. This does not mean that the parents must know how the child spends every dime. Rather, the child should be able to give account according to the general patterns of money management agreed upon.

When your child starts his first job, even if it is only mowing the neighbor's lawn or baby-sitting several hours in an evening, it is one step taking him in the direction of independence from you, his parents, and his home. Even though it raises questions, poses problems, creates dilemmas, it is a necessary step for the child. Give encouragement, help when needed, and do not hesitate to be definite about certain expectations that you consider basic.

Your child can be successful in his job if he has learned to accept responsibilities at home and developed skills in a variety of areas. If you can help your child work through the practical details of a job, related to transportation and family living around a work schedule, he will more easily remember that he lives not for himself alone but in relationship to other people. Helping your child find a sound pattern of money management gives him a needed survival skill for his approaching independence.

Someday his first job, or second, or another, will become a full-time, self-supporting job that takes him to the financial independence of his own apartment or household. Then you will be free to rearrange your life around his independence. It should be a good feeling, because that is the way it ought to be.

21

Pam Lamperelli and Jane Smith # When Your Child Gets Pregnant

"I'm pregnant!"

Carol looked at her daughter Susan's face. It's not true! she thought. I hear it, but I can't believe it. Not our little girl. She's only *fourteen.*

Wait a minute! It can't be! She's never had a date. Surely, there is a mistake. Lots of girls her age skip periods.

Yet looking at the pained, fearful expression on Susan's face, Carol knew it was true. Then her heart pounded and she felt a lump in her throat.

How do I tell her father? What will he think? What is my mother going to say? She and Dad idolize Susan. What will everyone else say? What did I do wrong? I have tried to be a good mother.

Suddenly Carol felt anger. *How could Susan do this to us? We have raised her better than this. We send her to private school. We have protected and sheltered her. We have saved to send her to college, and we had hopes that she would later pursue a career and travel. But now this.*

Pam Lamperelli, Pompano Beach, Florida, is a licensed clinical social worker in private practice for individual, marital, and family counseling. Jane M. Smith is Coordinator/Instructor of Human Sexuality for four private schools in Palm Beach County, Florida. As a counselor, she specializes in adolescent conflict and pregnancy cases.

Susan's expression brought Carol back to reality. She took her daughter into her arms and said, "We love you and we will work this out together."

When Susan's father was informed, he also felt anger, directed primarily toward the baby's father. He placed the entire blame on the boy, demanded to know who he was, and insisted that Susan never see him again. The more he pressed the issue, the more Susan silently withdrew from her parents.

Carol recognized what was happening and suggested that they first confirm the pregnancy at their local health department. When the nurse observed how distraught and confused the family was, she recommended that they contact the local pregnancy counseling agency.

The family made an appointment. Although the social worker was reassuring, all three family members were nervous, embarrassed, and wondered what her opinion of the family would be.

Susan was interviewed first. She was nonverbal, fidgety, and kept her eyes averted. She discussed how difficult and painful it was for her to tell her parents about this pregnancy.

The social worker learned that Susan had met the father of the baby through a chaperoned youth activity. She had never actually dated and did not accept being two months pregnant. Insisting that the act of intercourse had not been completed, her major concern seemed to be with missing school and her special social activities.

The interview with Susan's parents revealed that their normal loving and communicative relationship was under a great deal of stress. They suddenly felt inadequate as parents with additional feelings of anger, guilt, and shame. Alternately, they were blaming themselves and each other, and this blocked their communication. The social worker was supportive and reassured them that they were good parents, had done the best they knew how, and were not to blame. She then outlined some of the reasons for an out-of-wedlock pregnancy.

Among these was: "Pregnancy may result from a lack of knowledge about sexuality and sexual function." This seemed to be one of Susan's problems.

Susan's parents admitted that they may have had unreasonable expectations for Susan to be the "perfect" child. Her father said that since her puberty he has been uncomfortable with his role and definitely has been less than physically affectionate with his daughter. Although verbally affectionate, there was only superficial communication between father and daughter.

He also had a habit of being unavailable during a family crisis or during times of decision-making. He either found some errand to run, or he conveniently had to be out of the house or out of town on business.

Susan's parents insisted that termination of the pregnancy was out of the question. They expressed uncertainty as to keeping or surrendering the baby for adoption. They were reassured that they had a right to express their opinions. Because this baby was in fact their first grandchild, the decisions did involve them. However, the final decision would be Susan's.

Allowing someone else to make this decision for her would never afford Susan the opportunity to accept the responsibility for this pregnancy or the responsibility for her decision. She would also tend to blame others and allow them to become the brunt of her anger.

When the family was seen together, the social worker proceeded to explain what their program offered. There would be weekly counseling sessions with Susan, periodic sessions with her parents, and sessions together, as needed.

The father of the baby had to be involved because there is a U.S. Supreme Court law which dictates that, if a baby is surrendered for adoption, the named biological father must in fact surrender his rights to his child. He also has the right to deny paternity or appear in court and assert his rights to his child and provide the court with a plan for his child. Counseling is equally important for the baby's father. He too should be afforded the opportunity to accept responsibility for the pregnancy and to grow emotionally from the experience.

In the process of coping with her feelings about the pregnancy, Susan needed to work through her feelings toward the father of the baby. At this time, her parents objected to the father of her baby being involved in any way with Susan.

There would also be group sessions with other pregnant girls with the focus on accepting the pregnancy, discussing feelings and behaviors, and learning to improve their communication skills. Prenatal classes would instruct her about the pregnancy, delivery, physical and psychological development of the child, parenting skills, and child abuse. Human sexuality classes would focus on accurate facts about family planning and the importance of responsible sexual behavior.

The classes would also provide information about dealing with relationships, developing nonsexual communication skills, feelings about men and women and how to handle them, dating, assertiveness and learning how to say "no," and speaking up for one's rights in a positive way.

Susan had a choice of entering the maternity home at five months or staying with her family and continuing counseling. She chose the former. Her choice was *not* based on any desire to hide but on her desire to make her own decision and to cope with her reactions without the unnecessary pressures and criticisms from others. For Susan, this was an opportunity for her to have a place to grow.

Her parents were told that their role was essential in Susan's ability to decide and accept her decision. They had to learn to resolve their own feelings of anger, disappointment, and hurt if they were going to be able to provide Susan with the love, encouragement, and acceptance she would need.

Susan continued to go to school until her fifth month of pregnancy. During that period, she participated in counseling. She seemed preoccupied with seeing Tom, the father of her baby. In everything he did or said, she tried to convince herself that he loved her. She also expressed feelings of guilt. She was distraught at having hurt and disappointed her parents. She felt she wasn't any good, and she didn't deserve anything worthwhile.

Susan's parents revealed that they had severely restricted Susan's activities, keeping her isolated at home. They told Susan that she had made a grave mistake, and she needed to be punished. They also feared that she would seek further sexual activity. They began to demand that she keep the baby as a just punishment and a reminder of her error. This was a normal reaction for them, which arose from their anger, hurt, fears, and peer pressure from relatives and friends.

By her fifth month, Susan was beginning to show her pregnancy, and she entered the maternity home. She was able to continue her education with a homebound teacher provided by the local public school system. Around this time in her pregnancy, Susan was able to distinguish the baby's movements and began to recognize the baby as a separate part of her body. She was able to begin accepting the fact of her pregnancy. She was no longer able to deny the increasing physical evidence of it.

Susan bitterly questioned why this had to happen to her when several of her friends had actually completed the act of sexual intercourse more than once without becoming pregnant. Tom was unable to face the obvious evidence of her pregnancy and was therefore avoiding her. She felt angered by his lack of interest in her and their baby. Her anger was also due to his freedom to continue his life without having to face the emotional and physical consequences of this pregnancy.

She felt anger at the baby itself for forcing her to discontinue school with all her friends. She felt bitter about having to struggle to decide for their future, and she resented Tom's lack of concern for this responsibility.

Anger was expressed toward her parents and friends for pressuring her to keep the baby and toward her older siblings for pressuring her to surrender. The rejection of her baby was interpreted by Susan as an actual rejection of herself.

Susan's anger was occasionally vented at the social worker and other staff members. (Susan was angry because she had to suddenly face a difficult responsibility far in advance of her childish years.)

All of these feelings were freely expressed to and received with acceptance and support by the social worker and her staff. Being in the maternity home allowed Susan to be in an environment of total acceptance and warmth.

Because of her guilt, Susan put herself in punishing situations. She stayed by herself and made no effort to make friends. Her reluctance to follow the rules led the staff to frequently remind her of her responsibilities. Because her parents couldn't pick her up on one particular occasion, Susan assumed that they didn't care for her. She interpreted rejection in every relationship and lacked feelings of self-worth.

She became certain of having a difficult and painful labor and fantasized that there would be something wrong with the baby. All these things Susan felt would be just punishment for her. She deliberately ignored proper diet habits, neglected herself, and complained of being unable to sleep. She discontinued school because she didn't feel that she deserved an education. "Why bother?"

All of her behavior problems were a form of self-punishment to placate her guilt. When she was reminded of her "mistake" or made to feel guilty, her own guilt was reinforced and she responded with self-punishing behaviors. But what Susan needed now was support, love, and acceptance, *not* criticism.

Once Susan had accepted her pregnancy, she began to fantasize about being a mother and about having something of her very own. She spent her time imagining ways to support herself and to keep her child.

Her parents were encouraged to let her know to what degree they were able to support her emotionally and financially. Through counseling, they realized that they were unable and unprepared to take an infant into their home at this stage of their lives. Because of Susan's age and inexperience, the prime responsibility of child care would fall on them. With support, they were encouraged to follow through with their decision and to resolve their own guilt feelings for not accepting their grandchild into their home.

They needed to allow Susan to work out on her own a means of keeping her baby. So she contacted financial assistance agencies and various relatives, trying to arrange for a place for her to live with her baby.

She vacillated between keeping and surrendering her baby for several weeks. She expressed anger toward her parents for not allowing her to bring her baby home. On the other hand, she realized the decision was still hers to make.

Tom (the baby's father) also participated in counseling. He was encouraged to accept his share of the medical costs of the pregnancy.

At seven and a half months of pregnancy, Susan began childbirth classes. She gained confidence in dealing with her labor and delivery. At this point, she began to realize that she couldn't realistically raise her child by herself and provide all that she wanted for her child and herself. So once again, she was leaning toward surrender.

She began to withdraw, cried constantly, and slept most of the day. She was also intensely preoccupied with her impending loss and separation from her baby. During this period, which lasted approximately two weeks, Susan felt a deep despair and emptiness. To help her through the depression, she was encouraged to set new goals for herself, such as future plans for her education. She also had a need for reinvestment in her current relationships.

In group sessions she was encouraged to imagine the baby was out of her uterus and placed with a family. She had to face her feelings about this. Susan and the other members of her group participated in an exercise in which each girl pretended to be telling their baby how they felt, and why they decided either to keep or surrender.

Every woman who becomes pregnant has an idealized image of what her baby will look like, and what sex it will be. This fantasy baby is never born. In group exercises, Susan was encouraged to discuss her fantasy of her unborn child. Susan fantasized that her baby would be a girl and look just like Susan. (Many times when the girl has been rejected by the baby's father, her fantasy will exclude completely any characteristics of the biological father.)

These exercises may seem unduly painful, but they aid the unwed mother in ventilating her feelings of deep despair and loss and enhance her ability to accept the baby and have an emotional investment in her baby. If the girl is unable to participate, this can indicate that she is avoiding the grief and needs to work harder. Anticipatory grief prior to delivery is encouraged to help her prepare for the actual separation. The sense of loss and emotional reactions may not be as acute if anticipatory grief occurs. Susan was encouraged to share her experiences with her parents.

It is important at this time to emphasize to the girl's parents that they cannot fully get in touch with their daughter's experience of separation from her newborn. The parents, after the birth of their children, had nurtured them and thus bonded with them. They have a great emotional investment in their children. It is impossible, therefore, for them to fully get in touch with their daughter's experience of separating from her newborn. It is very important for parents to know this when their daughter approaches her delivery date.

The adoptive parent represents someone who takes away the baby, as well as someone who loves it. Parents who have adopted children were invited to the group sessions with students to discuss their side of the adoptive process. The adoptive worker was also invited to explain thoroughly the qualities of the foster parents and requirements of the foster homes. She also explained how prospective adoptive parents are screened and accepted.

Just prior to delivery, Susan became more confident with herself and with her ability to handle the loss and to follow through with her decision to surrender. As a result, she was anxious to deliver the baby and get on with plans for her future.

Susan gave Tom another opportunity to deal with the pregnancy and the decision to surrender. He chose not to be involved. He would be available to sign the necessary legal papers, but he did not want to see the baby. Susan was able to accept this as his choice, and she no longer interpreted it as personal rejection.

During a conference with her family, Susan told them how she wanted them to act toward her and the baby after she delivered. She wanted to be able to discuss her experience and her feelings with them.

Susan's labor progressed rapidly. A trained labor coach was available to be with Susan during her labor and delivery. She handled herself well, and her labor was uneventful. As she approached the pushing stage, Susan began to become tense and upset. Suddenly it occurred to her that once she delivered this baby, she would be like all other unwed mothers. It wouldn't matter that she had not completed the act of sexual intercourse. Now she was forced to face the reality that she was indeed having a baby out-of-wedlock. She also began to realize that once she pushed the baby out into the world, she would have to begin separating from him. The baby would no longer be safe inside her womb.

It was all happening so quickly. Susan began to panic. It was at this time that she completed her full acceptance of this pregnancy. Susan's labor coach praised her for how well she had been handling her labor. She was reminded of how well she had handled her previous weeks of counseling and classes. With gentle but firm encouragement, Susan was able to relax and began pushing. Within five minutes, Susan gave birth to a seven-pound baby boy.

Susan's immediate reaction was one of relief and pride in what she had done. She was also startled to realize that she did not give birth to her fantasy baby. This baby was very much an image of his biological father. Her idealized image was lost.

The hours that followed were happy ones for Susan. She received many fine compliments on her labor and delivery. She was proud of her handsome son, and everyone kept telling her how beautiful he was. She felt good, really good, about herself for the first time in months. She couldn't wait to call Tom to tell him about their son.

Once again, Tom chose not to see his child. Susan felt sorry for Tom for the first time since the onset of this pregnancy. He had missed so much by not seeing his child or being involved with plans for their baby. It was at this moment that she realized how very much this baby had given her.

She chose to name the baby Robert. This would be the name to be used by the foster mother and on the legal documents for the surrender. Susan was allowed to hold her baby under the supervision of her social worker. She had learned from counseling that she would be allowed to see and hold her baby with supervision, but that care would be taken to see that she did not bond with her baby. Being able to see the baby and dealing with her loss of her fantasy baby were most helpful in helping her to resolve her grief during the period of separation.

The first real separation for Susan was when she left the hospital, and the baby was received into foster care. It was helpful for her to know that she could see her baby again, and that the foster care papers which she signed were only temporary. She began to experience once again feelings of depression and despair.

The third to fifth post partum days were crucial for Susan. Her body was physically craving to complete the role of mothering. Her breasts began to prepare for the manufacture of milk in spite of the medication to prevent this. Her body suddenly ached from the rigors of labor and delivery, and she longed to hold her child.

She had been encouraged to stay at the maternity home for the first five days after she left the hospital. Susan was really glad that she had chosen to do so. The staff was supportive and right on hand to reaffirm all that she had learned in the previous weeks. She was allowed again to see her son with supervision and support.

Her family visited often and were kind and gentle. Her brothers and sisters were eager for her to return home. She was able to talk to her father and mother about her feelings.

Suddenly she became aware that she felt very, very close to her parents. She felt a peacefulness and security from her family which she had never experienced before. The warmth and love which she received from her family seemed to give her strength to deal with the difficult days ahead.

Sometime during the first six weeks after delivery, the final stages of separation took place. Tom signed the necessary legal documents. The day that Susan signed surrender papers represented still another moment of separation. Susan chose to see her baby for the last time on that day. She bought an outfit for him to wear the day he was placed with his adoptive parents. Susan also gave him a family keepsake as a token of her love. This gift would be passed on to the adoptive parents.

Susan's parents were invited to be with her when she signed her papers and saw the baby for the last time. This was extremely helpful for Susan because she would have someone who was close to her with whom to relate about her baby when she had the need.

Tom and Susan attended a private court hearing for permanent commitment of the baby to the adoption agency. The judge represented the authority who took away the baby, as well as being one who was concerned for the baby's welfare. A few days later the baby was placed with his adoptive parents.

General information about the family and the reactions of the baby and the parents on the day of his placement were shared with Susan and Tom. They were joyfully overwhelmed with Susan's gifts for the baby, and they promised to cherish the family keepsake for their son. These happy and positive bits of information will be a comfort to Susan forever.

22

Larry Kehler When Your Child
Gets a Driver's
License

"Okay, which one of you is it going to be?" Faye said with firm exasperation, keeping her eyes fixed on the road ahead. "I can't follow both your instructions."

Our daughter had just turned sixteen, and she had obtained her learner's permit for operating a car. We were returning home from a Sunday afternoon visit to friends, and she was getting her first experience in city driving. My wife in the backseat and I in the front were both giving Faye advice and throwing in little cautions, not all entirely compatible. It was on one occasion when we both were speaking at the same time that Faye blurted out that instruction was fine, but one instructor was all she could listen to. She had a good point, and we knew it.

After we relaxed a bit more, we were amazed at how quickly Faye caught on to the proper way of driving. She oversteered at first and tended to drive with the right wheels on the white line, but she soon corrected these errors.

Later that evening my wife, Jessie, and I both recalled the nerve-racking times we had had getting accustomed to city

Larry Kehler, Winnipeg, Manitoba, and his wife Jessie (Neufeld) are parents of two grown children, Daryl and Faye. Larry is general secretary of the Conference of Mennonites in Canada.

135

driving. We had learned to drive in the country and in small towns. The prospect of driving an automobile in the "big city" had looked ominously impossible to us. We developed "emotional blocks" which made our first driving experience on city streets much more traumatic than it need have been.

But in just a matter of days Faye was driving along Portage Avenue, Winnipeg's busiest thoroughfare, during rush hours, without getting flustered. I was the nervous one, trying to guide the car with disguised body contortions and foot action. I tried to sound calm and assured as I gave instructions on where she was to drive and how she could improve her technique.

My nervousness was misplaced. Faye had a good sense of the road and of the vehicle she was driving. We had allowed her to do a bit of illicit driving on deserted country roads and on a nearby parking lot before she turned sixteen, but I was surprised at the quickness with which she picked up the "real thing."

Faye had none of the hang-ups Jessie and I had about driving being "nervous time" or that it was really a "manly" activity, one which women could never do quite right. In fact, it was overconfidence rather than a lack of it against which we had to warn. Faye tended to drive aggressively almost from the start. So we stressed the importance of defensive driving.

So now Faye was about ready for her road test. In our city, the examination which determined whether or not she's qualified to be issued a driver's license was a rigid one. Many people failed their first and second tries. She was calm about it; we were biting our nails.

Sitting at the testing office, waiting for the car to return from the road test was harder than taking the test. We knew because we had been through it once before.

Two years ago when our son Daryl reached sixteen he had

wanted to see how quickly he could pass through the "learner" stage. Several days every week we took practice drives with him. We drove the route on which the tester would likely be taking him. We rehearsed parallel parking between garbage cans set along the curb in front of our house. When we thought he was off to a good start, he was already announcing his intention to take the test.

"Oh, well," we thought, "even if he fails, as he is likely to, it will be a good experience for him. He'll know next time what the tester is really looking for."

The one concession we had made to a driver's education program was to ask a nephew who had just received training as a driving instructor to take Daryl out for a few hours before the test. Aside from this, we did the training ourselves, adhering closely to the manual issued by the provincial motor vehicles department.

My wife took him to the test. I was at work that day, but I worried about how he would do. I was anxious about what the phone call from them would say. My expectations were that Jessie would report, "He did quite well but not well enough."

When she finally did call, she made it all sound so matter-of-fact. "He had seven points charged against him," she announced.

"How many are they allowed?" I pushed.

"Fifty."

"Fifty! Then he made it easily. That's great!"

We had wanted to celebrate a bit as a family that night, but Daryl couldn't make it. "Dad, could I have the car tonight?"

So a new phase had begun in our life as a family.

Now we had to go through all the pangs which accompany the birth of a new driver, again. Faye eventually passed her tests and, like millions of others, is driving on our highways.

Jessie and I don't make any claims to being above average in our driving abilities, but we have tried to set good examples for our children. We adhere, although not slavishly, to traffic regulations; we try to drive defensively; and we admit our mistakes frankly to each other when we make them. We also point out errors that we notice other people making on the road. We hope this approach will have a positive influence on the way Daryl and Faye drive.

We have no quarrel with the driver education programs in our schools. Our children simply weren't ready to wait several months until the next course was available. And we weren't quite prepared to pay the high fees which commercial driving schools charge.

Perhaps in no other place is North American individualism more evident than on Canadian and U.S. roads. The prevailing spirit is to claim as much of the street or highway for ourselves as we can and to honk, glower, or sideswipe anyone who dares to impede our progress. There are not many places where it is as difficult to practice the Christian virtue of patience and of "you first" as it is on our roadways. When we help our children to learn the art of driving, we also need to provide an alternative to the "me first" attitude which seems to be an unwritten law of the road.

23

Hope Lind When Your Child Goes Away to College

In a sudden whirl, she was off, running to keep up with the ticket agent hustling her and her cello on the plane ahead of the other passengers. There wasn't even time for decent good-byes. We strained our eyes against the darkness, wondering if that was her plane that we saw, heading toward the early morning hours in Indiana.

Our daughter Janet was off to Goshen College, and we were left behind with letters to write and bills to pay. If your family is like ours, there is nothing unusual about writing letters and paying bills, per se. But they take on new dimensions with a college student. And being left behind when your child goes away to college separates you more distinctly and with a kind of finality that earlier, shorter separations did not have.

No longer do you know when your child gets up in the morning, who most of her friends are, what her textbooks look like, what she does with her free time, when she goes to bed—unless she chooses to tell you. Our daughter didn't live with us anymore, except for vacations. She had moved out of our everyday lives. She became independent, responsible for

Hope Lind, Eugene, Oregon, and her husband Cliff are the parents of Janet, Myron, Julia, and Carl. Hope frequently reviews books and is writing a history of Oregon Mennonites.

herself, making her own decisions in a way she was not doing before going away to college.

It was part of her transition to adulthood. My husband, Cliff, and I believe that for her own maturation our being left behind was necessary. We wanted our high school children to live with us, at home. But we have been quite willing for our college children to leave.

Even so, we have missed our daughter's cheery whistling of themes from symphonies and our son's vivid accounts of bicycle races. Maybe we didn't miss two hours a day of scales and arpeggios and other piano practicing in the living room, or the emptying of the cookie jar's quadruple batch of chocolate chip cookies in five days. Life soon took on a new normalcy, and there was no need to feel guilty about enjoying new freedoms made possible with the departure of our student.

One friend said to me, after her college daughter left, "It seems so weird to think that she is gone, and yet our life goes on just like it did before." Now, with her college children living away from home, she is able to enjoy a more relaxed schedule.

This is the time for "background parenting," just *being there* (even if the background is half a continent away), a sounding board for dropping a class or staying an extra college term. Your student needs the security of knowing he's not entirely on his own, not quite yet. He or she knows that parents are available, if something urgent should arise. ("Hello." "Will you accept a collect call?")

But it's good to provide tangible evidence. We do occasionally talk with our college student by telephone, but letter writing fits our style and budget better, and it's easier to schedule.

Before Janet went away for her first year of college, her

father told her that if she would address and stamp envelopes for him and get them together in a box with paper, he would write to her every week. Knowing her father's correspondence disinclinations, Janet was amazed that he would even suggest such a thing. And when his weekly letters landed in her mailbox, they told her as much as did their contents that his love and concern and openness to her are deep.

I, too, write frequently to our students, usually enclosing a church bulletin and sometimes a cartoon (especially of Heathcliff and his misadventures with the trombone) or a newspaper clipping about family or friends. We try to avoid the urge to preach, but once in a while some unsolicited advice does slip through.

Our college students may not always write as often as we'd like, but we know that doesn't mean they love us less. Rather, college students are often wrapped up in their own affairs and are usually quite busy. (Remember how it was when *you* were in college!) Their world is expanding to include new friends, and there just is not as much time for family.

Write to your student anyway. Call now and then. Send a care package, if you like. Do remind your student, in various ways with no strings attached, that you love and care.

Being left behind with college bills can cause parents to go into shock if they haven't given forethought to the matter. For our family, going away to college implies attending one of our church colleges. But the cost of choosing a Mennonite or other private college is much higher than it would be at the state university near our home.

We were introduced to the dilemma of financing college costs when Janet was a high school senior. Although we knew vaguely that costs had accelerated since our college days, we knew next to nothing about financing a college education in terms of this generation. When we filled out the detailed application for financial aid, as the school counselor encouraged all parents to do, we learned some startling facts: families of medium income who own their homes or farms, and have lived modestly in order to save and invest for future needs, have more difficulty qualifying for financial aid than families at the same income level who have chosen to live more luxuriously, spent freely, and saved or invested little. So much for financial aid.

For Cliff and me, helping our children with their college costs is intended to affirm our support for them and our willingness to invest in their future. However, we feel that even if we were able to pay for all their college expenses, we would still make them responsible for part of their costs to help them in the process of becoming independent adults. The percentage of their education costs that we pay varies from child to child, depending upon earning power during their high school and college years. It has been no more than half and no less than one third. And they have had to borrow money.

Two years after Janet left for Goshen, with a college-bound son, we discovered another dimension to having a child go away to college.

"Dad," said Myron, "we'd better begin thinking about getting a new car. I need to take the VW bus to college."

Up to then, our children had not asked for cars or wanted to buy their own. Our 1968 VW bus and the Datsun pickup one year newer sometimes sat in the garage for days at a time, while our family bicycled five, eight, ten, twelve miles to school, work, or church. But was there validity in Myron's request for a car for transportation to college?

We estimated fares from Oregon to a church college and home again. We estimated costs of driving—gasoline, oil, food, motel, insurance, time, arbitrary allowance for unknowns that could develop with an elderly car. Yes, there would be some financial advantage in taking a car, if you didn't include its purchase price.

There are other things to consider when your child goes away to college, like the hurts you share with your student—at a distance—at times of homesickness, illness, injury, or stress. It is at such times that we have been especially thankful for the caring Christian people who step forward with support and help.

From our experience, several themes keep popping up when we think about children going away to college:

1. *Assess family finances well ahead of time* and begin budgeting or making other arrangements for meeting college costs.

2. *Keep in touch with your student* in specific, scheduled ways. Everybody, including the away-at-college child, needs concrete reminders of love from parents and other important people.

3. *Be available in the background* for those special, unexpected needs and joys.

4. *Pray.* For compatible roommate, trustworthy friends, appropriate vocational decisions, all those important things that you can no longer do anything else about. Before your child leaves, while he or she is there, all the time!

And when your child comes home for Christmas or summer vacation, expect to meet someone who has changed, grown—a flower now in blossom. There may be thorns for those who would grasp the flower, but parents who can give freedom for it to open more fully can expect to stand back and muse, "Isn't she becoming a lovely person?" "Hasn't he matured a lot?" It should be worth being left behind with letters to write and bills to pay.

24

Kenneth L. Gibble ## When Your Child Gets a Divorce

Scene I: The inside of a church, the bride in white, surrounded by nervous bridesmaids, the groom ill-at-ease but obviously happy, the minister telling the couple to love and cherish each other, the vows spoken quietly but with conviction—"to have and to hold from this day forward . . . for better, for worse . . . till death do us part." Then smiles, laughter, flashbulbs popping, tearful embraces.

Scene II: Three years or seven years or fifteen years later. The telephone rings and the familiar voice at the other end of the line says: "Dad, I know this is going to be hard for you and Mom, but Joe and I have decided to get a divorce."

Those two scenes, or something very much like them, occur more and more these days. It is the rare family that is not touched by divorce at some point. For people who have had a family and religious tradition of the sanctity of marriage, the increasing frequency of divorces is especially painful. The pain becomes particularly acute when parents see their own children through a divorce.

Parents' reactions vary because each situation is different.

Kenneth L. Gibble and his wife Ann copastor the Arlington, Virginia, Church of the Brethren, and are parents of Katie. Kenneth's articles have appeared in more than 70 different magazines. He is author of five books and of several plays.

144

Some parents are mortified by the thought of a divorce in their family. "What will our friends think? What will we say to people at church?" They see their child's divorce as a bad reflection on their parenting or even on their own marriage.

Other parents react by expressing strong feelings of anger—often toward their child's spouse, on whom they place the major blame—but sometimes towards their own child. This anger may take the form of bitter recriminations or cold, silent withdrawal.

I have known some parents who were grief-stricken when they learned of their child's divorce. They may have had genuine affection for their son- or daughter-in-law. The loss of that relationship is painful to them, especially if it is combined with separation from grandchildren.

And, finally, there are some parents who are overjoyed at the prospect of their child's divorce: "I always said she wasn't good enough for our son." "He was making our daughter's life miserable—getting away from him will be the best thing that ever happened to her."

One response I have almost never encountered on the part of parents is that of indifference. Because of the heavy emotional investment most mothers and fathers have in their children's lives, they cannot help but be deeply affected by a broken marriage, even if the children have been away from home for many years. If grandchildren are involved, a divorce is even more traumatic.

Thus parents whose children get divorced should give attention to two important things: (1) their response to the ones actually going through the divorce and (2) their response to their own feelings and their own marriage relationship.

What are the most helpful responses parents can make to their divorced children? To answer this question, I have drawn upon conversations with divorced persons in my congregation and community. In various ways, each of them indicated what they needed and what they did *not* need from their parents at this difficult period in their lives.

1. *People getting a divorce don't need a lecture on the sanctity of marriage.* Parents sometimes hope that by reminding their child of the vows he or she made during the wedding ceremony a divorce can be prevented. This "reminder" may take the form of a parental sermon on what the Bible teaches about divorce, a summary of what the preacher said recently about the importance of strong marriages, etc. The one going through the divorce has almost certainly been struggling with these issues and knows exactly how parents feel about them.

2. *Persons getting divorced do not need emotional outbursts from their parents.* I have sometimes had people tell me, "I can't talk to my mother and father about the breakup of my marriage. I know Mother will start crying and Dad will throw a temper tantrum." While parents should not attempt to bottle up their emotions, they do their child a disservice by giving vent to these emotions while the child is present. A person going through a divorce is likely already dealing with all the emotional freight he or she can safely handle. Rather than risk taking more on themselves than they can manage, many will simply avoid their parents. Thus a potentially helpful means of support is lost to them.

3. *Another thing persons getting divorced do not need from their parents is meddling.* By "meddling," divorced persons often mean actions such as taking sides, calling the estranged partner on the phone to try to convince him or her to reconsider, urging the minister to "talk some sense into those two," or similar attempts to bring matters to what the parents

regard as a satisfactory conclusion. Yes, it is tempting for Mother and Dad, who have spent much of their lives "knowing what is best for our child," to take up that role again during such a traumatic time. But parents' interference during a divorce nearly always causes resentment on the part of one or both members of the separated couple. Parents have sometimes managed to get a couple "reconciled" only to learn that the conflicts causing the problem are still not resolved. What follows can only be more hostility and heartbreak.

However, I do not mean to imply that parents should declare a completely "hands off" policy during a divorce. Ignoring the situation, pretending that nothing is amiss, is of no help to anyone. What a child *does* need from parents is understanding and concern, and these can both be offered without trying to influence the outcome of the couple's marital problems.

I once had someone tell me, "I know my parents are deeply upset because Jenny and I are separated, but I also know they aren't going to try to manipulate either her or me. The other night Dad said simply: 'Phil, we love you and Jenny. You can count on our love and support no matter what decision you finally reach.' " The young man who said that was tremendously grateful for his parents' support. It gave him the confidence he needed to make what were, in the long run, the best choices for himself and his former wife. If parents can relate to their children as adults who are competent to run their own lives, they can feel free to be as helpful and supportive in whatever way their child asks.

If there are children in the family of a divorcing couple, they will need the ongoing love of their grandparents. Grandparents are sometimes tempted to go overboard at such times, in an effort to compensate for the loss grandchildren may be feeling. Rather than overdoing it, grandparents should follow their usual pattern of relating to the grandchildren at such a time. This itself will reassure the youngsters that life is still orderly, that the difficulties their parents are having will not mean the loss of their relationship with their grandparents.

There are two other things parents can do for their children during a time of divorce. One is to recommend professional counseling if it has not been tried. Whether reconciliation is a possibility or not, counseling can be of great help for the person having to adjust to a new and difficult life situation. The second thing parents can do is to pray—for their child, their child's spouse, and for grandchildren. Children who know their parents are praying for them treasure this kind of support, if they believe the prayers are offered in a spirit of wanting whatever is best for all concerned.

And while parents will naturally be concerned about the welfare of their child during a time of divorce, they ought also give attention to their own needs. Surely one of the most important of those is to be able to express feelings to someone who will be understanding and supportive. Guilt, anger, disappointment are only a few of the feelings that parents may have. Being able to talk with a good friend about them can be a tremendous help.

I have known parents who were so ashamed of their child's divorce that they withdrew from their friends and church acquaintances. The loneliness that resulted, even though self-imposed, was an added weight they certainly did not need. It may be important for parents who are troubled by their child's divorce to talk with their minister or with a professional counselor. In this setting they may be free to express their bottled-up feelings. Such counsel can be assist them in determining the most helpful responses they can make to a divorced couple.

A child's divorce can place strain on the parents' marriage.

Parents will naturally be thinking about the meaning of a marriage commitment at such a time. Why not use it, then, as an occasion for reaffirmation of one's own marriage vows? This can be done during times of quiet conversation between the spouses, as they reflect on what they have experienced together in the past and what their hopes are for the future. Such attention to their own marriage should not be done out of panic—"if we aren't careful, *our* marriage will fall apart"—but out of a renewed appreciation for each other and an intention to keep growing in their relationship.

Divorce, as painful as it is, need not condemn people to despair. Approached in a spirit of humility, it can actually be an opportunity for self-understanding and growth, both for the couple going through the divorce, and for their parents.

25

Harold L. Bussell When Your Child
Goes Astray

Two parents sat across from me, two who for a decade had
lived under tremendous guilt. They had struggled with feelings
of spiritual bankruptcy and for this reason had not been active
in church for five years. I had known this couple for over 20;
they were quality parents, consistent, faithful to God, yet they
were spiritually and emotionally disabled. Why?

Ten years earlier, their son had turned his back on the
Christian faith, his wife, and family, and had opted for the glit-
ter and tinsel of the jet set. Then five years ago the parents attended a family seminar in their church and were taught that if
parents just have the right order, claim the right Bible verses,
and model the ideal Christian example, God promises not to
let their children depart from the faith. Obviously, these
parents determined, their son's departure was their fault—
perhaps some secret sin, neglected quiet times, a failure to wit-
ness enough or to give generously to missions.

Many quality Christian parents find themselves in the same
position—discouraged, broken, guilt-ridden, and ultimately
withdrawn from others because of what their children have

Harold Bussell has been dean of the chapel at Gordon College, Wenham, Massa-
chusetts, since 1976. His most recent book is *Lord, I Can Resist Anything but Tempta-
tion* (Zondervan). Harold and his wife Carol are the parents of Monique and Brad-
ford.

done. How easily we forget that all the children of God went astray! We overlook the fact that Cain and Abel were raised in the same home, and yet one turned sour.

Basic to the problem of wayward children and parents' reactions is a secular view of the person to which many Christians have subscribed—and that view is often baptized with Bible verse taken out of context. The world sees the human being as a higher animal, a machine conditioned by environment. Create the right environment, it says, and you will produce the right products. Design a reward and punishment system, and you will produce all the same responses.

Does that sound familiar? Get the right chain of command in the home, put in the right cassette, attend a certain workshop, never miss devotions, and all will be well.

The Bible, however, does not present such a simplistic view of life. Human beings are made in the image of a complex God. That fact, coupled with the effects of the fall, the influence of the world, and unseen spiritual battles waging around us, makes simplistic answers seem strangely inadequate. These factors influence even the most solid Christian homes.

So what should be the perspective of parents coping with a child who has gone astray?

1. *We need to see teaching on the family within the context of all of Scripture.* We need to ask if our teaching views a person only as a machine, conditioned only by right environments, Bible verses, quiet times, and seminars.

2. *Prayer for and ministry to our children must acknowledge a biblical perspective of time.* God does not always answer prayer in our time framework. Jesus spent three years with his disciples, and they still doubted when he commissioned them

(Mt. 28:16-17). A three-day seminar will not solve all problems in parenting.

Consider the struggles Moses' mother must have faced. She had invested her life in this young miracle, had seen God deliver him and provide the best training for him. And the first thing Moses did after identifying with God's people was commit murder and run. How embarrassing!

He was not even seen for another 40 years. There were no verses to claim (the Bible hadn't been written yet), no seminars to attend, no telephone hot lines to call, not even a cassette ministry to help! Moses disappeared for 40 years and was 40 when he ran. Chances are his mother never saw the answer to her prayers. She could easily have questioned her investment in this gift of God.

But encouragement and hope are to be found in a sovereign God. God knew where Moses went. He raised up another family to minister to him and did not discard Moses because of his earlier failures. If your child has strayed, God knows where he or she is and knows that child by name.

3. *When a child strays, parents struggle with tremendous hurts, pain, and embarrassment.* As members of the body of Christ we need to be sensitive to the feelings of parents with wayward children. We need to withhold judgment and remember that we do not and never will understand all of the factors involved.

Certainly if there have been failures they need to be confessed and dealt with so that parents can move on in ministry toward others. But our responsibility is to "weep with those who weep" (Rom. 12:15, NASB), sharing God's comfort in that way. Such experiences of pain can be a tremendous source of encouragement and healing for others facing crises.

4. *Parents often feel that if they had just had enough faith their child would not have strayed.* Hurting parents need to be reminded that Scripture never deals with what could have been but shows God's sovereign grace coming to grips with the raw edges of reality.

There is no need for God's grace in ideal situations. However, realistic Christians face real circumstances affected by the fall, Satan, the world, and other Christians; they are in need of God's grace daily. In the midst of these struggles we are called not to have great faith in God but to have faith in a great God.

Christ's strength is made perfect in our weakness, not our success. Parents who struggle with feelings of guilt and condemnation do not need more platitudes and simplistic answers. They need Christian friends who will let them express their feelings, who can cry with them and pray with them. They need friends who will demonstrate incarnational caring.

Other Resources on Family Life

And Then There Were Three by Sara Wenger Shenk. A young woman shares the profound adjustments motherhood brings into her life. 224 pages.

The Fifteen Most Asked Questions About Adoption by Laura Valenti. A simple, honest approach that gives prospective adopters a clear preview of the steps ahead. 224 pages.

Good Thoughts at Bedtime, helps children forget nighttime fears and loneliness; *Good Thoughts About Me,* encourages feelings of self-worth; *Good Thoughts About People,* builds positive attitudes and respect for others—oversize picture books, text by Jane Hoober Peifer, photographs by Marilyn Peifer Nolt. 24 pages each.

Helping Children Cope with Death by Robert V. Dodd. Observations by an experienced pastor. 56 pages.

How to Teach Peace to Children by J. Lorne Peachey. Twenty-one specific ideas that anyone can use. 32 pages.

Inside and Occupied by Nancy S. Williamson. Over 500 projects for parents of children who have "nothing to do." 192 pages.

Lord, Help Me Love My Sister by Clair G. Cosby. Twenty-one sets of prayers by junior high sisters as they view both sides of the same experience.   80 pages.

Meditations for the New Mother by Helen Good Brenneman. The classic collection of daily reflections for the first 30 days after the birth of a child. More than 380,000 copies in print. 78 pages.

Renewing Family Life by Abraham and Dorothy Schmitt. Presents each stage of courtship, marriage, and parenthood as an opportunity for growth and fulfillment.   136 pages.

Seven Things Children Need by John M. Drescher. Significance, security, acceptance, love, praise, discipline, and God. 152 pages.

Tell Me About Death, Mommy by Janette Klopfenstein. A young widow shares from her own experience how to help children come to terms with the death of a loved one.   112 pages.

These books are available from your local bookstore or from Herald Press, Scottdale, Pa. 15683-1999 or Kitchener, Ont. N2G 4M5.